Forsaking all for Christ

a biography of

Henry Martyn

The First Modern Pioneer-Missionary to the Muslims

Henry Martyn (1781-1812)
Henry at the age of 24. He sat for this picture on 8 July 1805.

'For though I preach the gospel, I have nothing to glory of: for necessity is laid upon me; yea, woe is unto me, if I preach not the gospel!'
1 Cor. 9:16

Forsaking all for Christ

a biography of

Henry Martyn

The First Modern Pioneer-Missionary to the Muslims

Compiled from reliable sources
chiefly by

B V HENRY

With a foreword by George Verwer

CHAPTER TWO
London

Forsaking all for Christ, a biography of Henry Martyn, The First Modern Pioneer-Missionary to the Muslims compiled from reliable sources chiefly by B V Henry
Copyright © 2003 B. V. Henry
The text of this book © 2007 Chapter Two Trust, London
ISBN 978 1 85307 229 1 hardback
Originally published in German in 2003, Swedish edition 2007

All rights reserved. No part of this publication may be reproduced or transmitted in any form or by any means, electronic or mechanical, including photocopying, recording, or storage in any information retrieval system, without written permission from Chapter Two.

Chapter Two, Fountain House, Conduit Mews, London SE18 7AP
www.chaptertwobooks.org.uk, e-mail chapter2uk@aol.com

Distributors:
- Bible, Book and Tract Depot, 23 Santarosa Avenue, Ryde, NSW 2112, Australia
- Believers Bookshelf, 5205 Regional Road 81, Unit 3, Beamsville, ON, L0R 1B3, Canada
- Bible Treasury Bookstore, 46 Queen Street, Dartmouth, Nova Scotia, B2Y 1G1, Canada
- El-Ekhwa Library, 3 Anga Hanem Street, Shoubra, Cairo, Egypt
- Bibles & Publications Chrétiennes, 30 rue Châteauvert, 26000 Valence, France
- CSV, An der Schloßfabrik 30, 42499 Hückeswagen, Germany
- Christian Truth Bookroom, Paddisonpet, Tenali 522 201, Andhra Pradesh, India
- Words of Life Trust, 3 Chuim, Khar, Mumbai, 400 052, India
- Words of Truth, 38-P.D.A Lamphelpat, Imphal 795 004, Manipur, India
- Uit het Woord der Waarheid, Postbox 260, 7120AG Aalten, Netherlands
- T&T, 25 Sharnbrook Lane, Regent's Park, Christchurch 8051, New Zealand
- Echoes of Truth, No 11 Post office road, P.O. Box 2637, Mushin, Lagos, Nigeria
- Kristen Litteratur, Heiloveien 3, 4353 Klepp Stasjon, Norway
- Grace & Truth Book-room, 87 Chausee Road, Castries, St. Lucia, WI
- Chapter Two S.A., P.O. Box 83645, South Hills, 2136, South Africa
- Beröa Verlag, Zellerstrasse 61, 8038 Zürich, Switzerland
- Éditions Bibles et Littérature Chrétienne, La Foge C, Case Postale, 1816 Chailly-Montreux, Switzerland
- Chapter Two Bookshop, 199 Plumstead Common Road, London, SE18 2UJ, UK
- Holdfast Bible & Tract Depôt, 41York Road, Tunbridge Wells, Kent, TN1 1JX, UK
- Words of Truth, PO Box 147, Belfast, BT8 4TT, Northern Ireland, UK
- Believers Bookshelf Inc., Box 261, Sunbury, PA 17801, USA
- Chapter Two Books USA, P.O.B. 400737, North Cambridge, MA, 02140, USA
- Bible House, PO Box 344G, St George, Barbados, WI

Printed in Holland

CONTENTS

The Genesis of this Book	9
Publisher's Note	10
Foreword by George Verwer	11
Prologue	13
1 The Change that Made a Difference	15
Early Years	
Godly Influences	
Decision and Opposition	
Vocation and Preparation	
2 The Cost of Total Commitment	40
Miss Lydia Grenfell	
Farewell to the Dearest	
Separation without Detachment	
3 That All May Know and Believe	54
Sea Voyage to India	
Arrival at Calcutta	
Acquaintance with William Carey	
Assignment to Dinapore	
Top Missionary Priority	
4 Triumphing Over Adversities	81
Fateful Transfer to Cawnpore	
Mrs Mary Sherwood's Impressions	
Excitement and Reservation	

5 The Strong Urge of his Soul 93
   Recommendation and Consideration
   New Horizons: Arabia and Persia
   Ten Month's Residence in Shiraz
   Confessor and Contender for the Christian Faith
   Jubilant Release: The Persian New Testament

6 His Unfulfilled Longings 116
   Return to England: Anticipation and Apprehension
   Journey into Turkey: The Beginning of the End

7 The Impact of his Life 128
   Institutional Memorials
   Written Records
   Burden and Vision
   Intellectual Achievements
   Testimony and Tribute

Epilogue: Though Dead he Speaks …............................. 153

Maps 155
Bibliography and other reference sources 157

Index 164

This book is dedicated to the memory of
Charles and Pearl Marsh,
former missionaries in Algeria from 1925 to 1962

THE GENESIS OF THIS BOOK

It was at an early stage of my Christian life, in England on a journey to Ireland, that I came across the name of Henry Martyn again. I had heard him spoken about several times previously and with great passion when I was involved with the youth movement of Operation Mobilisation in continental Europe.

A young and keen George Verwer often referred to him at meetings while his more sober and senior fellow-speaker, William MacDonald, frequently quoted him. Then, finding and reading an old biography in Dublin sparked my interest even more to get to know about his life and ministry. I therefore decided to embark on a quest to retrace his missionary travels from Cambridge to Tokat, collecting as much information as I could from written records and other sources in India, Persia, Turkey, Arabia and England.

Though a number of biographers have written about Henry Martyn over the past 200 years and there are references to him in many mission history books, the current generation of Christians knows very little about this 'meteor' in the dark sky of the Islamic world. I was so fascinated by this guiding light, among other stars of unsung missionary heroes (he was young – about my age when I discovered him – and full of ambition), that I made it one of my goals to revive his memory and legacy. It took many years to assemble this material.

This biography, like my other ones, is a sort of synthesis of previous books with additional information and insight, written not only from an historical, but also a spiritual, point of view. Although meant for personal reading, this new study has been structured in a similar way to the previous one so that it might also be used in Bible and mission schools as a text-book.

BVH

PUBLISHER'S NOTE

Henry Martyn is a significant character in church history because of the pioneering motivation that led him to reach out to the Muslim.

His foresighted endeavours made him the pioneer in this field. His work was a stimulus to men like A N Groves (1795-1853), Edward Cronin (1801-1882) John V Purnell (Lord Congleton) (1805-1883), the younger brother of John Henry Newman, Francis W Newman (1805-1897), and Dr. John Kitto (1804-1854) who devoted themselves to 'faith missionary' work. The revival of interest in missionary endeavours in the early 1800s did not wane. American Presbyterians went to the Middle East, among whom were A H Rule (1843-1906) and B F Pinkerton (1838-1890) who laboured in Egypt and Syria. The latter was especially used of God in the formation of many Christian assemblies. There are now over 200 such assemblies in Egypt and in neighbouring countries.

God uses one man in a special way and much fruit follows. This interesting biography gives the story and it is the publisher's wish that the reader will be stimulated to serve the Lord more diligently in this needy world.

E N Cross
April 2007

FOREWORD

Surely this is one of the most important and relevant biographies in the history of missions. A previous, smaller biography of Henry Martyn made an impact on me, and so I was excited to see this more extensive presentation. I also found the other biographical sketches of people like David Brainerd and Charles Simeon very interesting.

I pray that God will use this book to increase interest in the Muslim world, which is still the greatest challenge facing the church of Jesus Christ.

Would you help get this important book into the hands of others? Let's work and pray to get this into church libraries and other libraries wherever we can.

We are burdened for the Muslim people who live in our midst, and we need great action to demonstrate the love of Christ to them. Without Christian people who will commit themselves to 'go the extra mile,' we will never fulfil the Great Commission.

George Verwer

The last portrait of Henry Martyn
This was painted in Calcutta in 1810. Henry was always conscious of his physical frailty, and knew only too well that he was unlikely to live for many years. This overshadowing and sobering consideration may not only account for a certain melancholy 'pale cast of thought' but also for a burning urgency in intense and heroic endeavour to accomplish the most in a limited time.

PROLOGUE

This is designed to be a sympathetic but convincing narrative of a Christian born in Georgian England towards the end of the 18th century, who died in the flower of his age, at 31, far away from his native country. His story needs to be retold and is written with the hope that the flame which animated and consumed his life as a fragrant sacrifice for his Master might be rekindled in a new generation, and that Muslims might know and believe the gospel message.

Motherless from childhood, Henry was brought up in the spiritual atmosphere that resulted from a sweeping revival across England. With his precocious aptitude for study, he attended Cambridge University where his brilliance was recognised and acclaimed. It was during that period of education that the temperamental and impulsive young man was touched by God's grace through the crisis of another bereavement, and that his conversion led to a turning away from his own selfish ambitions.

Although a promising academic career lay before him and the prospect of what may have been a happy marriage, Henry came to renounce the legitimate things usually sought by most to follow what he strongly felt to be God's calling for his life. He made a definite decision to direct his whole attention to the spiritual needs of the East and to become a tool in God's hands.

He was active overseas in service in India and Persia for no longer than six years, in weak health and deprivation. But in the midst of indifference and hostility, he accomplished by his godly example and persevering efforts lasting results and blessings that are still felt long after his premature death from tuberculosis in north-eastern Turkey.

This confessor of faith has passed away, but he has left us the passion and vision that were his to be a living witness to Muslims. Indeed India and Persia where he stayed, and Arabia which he visited for a short time, remain mission-fields of great spiritual need in our days. The opportunities to labour are much better now, and yet they still require that devotion to the Lord and commitment which marked Henry's life and service. His legacy is not to be neglected if we are to labour at this very demanding task.

Writing this book has required research using information that was not always easy to find. It has also involved a number of journeys in the West and East to make various enquiries to produce what I hope is a true historical and psychological portrait of Henry Martyn and an accurate description of his environment. It also makes brief references to persons who directly or indirectly influenced his life and achievements.

The book is more than a mere historical or biographical sketch. It is also an exposition of unchanging truths and timeless principles which call for personal reflection and self-examination. If this goal is reached, the book fulfils its purpose of inspiration and motivation for fuller consecration.

'Believing, loving, serving' – ever learning as His disciple –
Ps. 90:12 & 2 Tim. 3:14

B V Henry, Hultafors, Sweden
Autumn 2005

1

THE CHANGE THAT MADE A DIFFERENCE

Early Years

The life of Henry Martyn, which ended at the early age of 31, commenced in a tin mine owner's family in Truro, the principal city in the county of Cornwall in the south-west peninsula of England. Henry, born on 18 February 1781, was the son of John Martyn's second wife, who died when her son was only two years old. The tuberculosis that killed her and Henry's two married sisters, Laura (born 1779) and Sally (born 1782), was evident in him and was the likely cause of his untimely death as well.

Truro in the 18th century – 'the place of memory'

John Martyn was a prudent father who brought up his motherless family of four children – John, the eldest of them, was born in 1766 – with unselfish devotion. He was a man who had been engaged in commercial pursuits, but who had also been deeply affected by the new spiritual awakening under the powerful preaching of John Wesley (1703-1791) then stirring England. He could not leave his children unaffected by his own personal experience of the goodness of God (see Rom. 2:4; 2 Cor. 7:10). It is most likely that John took his eight-year-old son with him to hear John Wesley's last sermon in Truro in 1789. Yet in his early years, Henry seems to have shown little or no interest in regular church-going or biblical studies, and as a teenager took the part of a free-thinker to the chagrin of his very pious sister, Sally. He certainly gave no sign of a religious inclination until he reached the age of 18.

When he was seven, a good-humoured and alert lad, Henry entered the local Truro Grammar School under the care of Dr. Cornelius Cardew, and proved to be a clever if not always diligent pupil. In October 1797 the studious teenager left home for the first time, to go up to St. John's College, Cambridge, to the delight and pride of his father who did not have the privilege of being highly educated. Valuing such education as few in England did at that time, John Martyn had always encouraged his son to think of taking a university course. Henry realised his debt to his father, both financial and educational, and he was determined to undertake his studies as well as he could for his father's sake as much as his own. Although up to that time his education had been entirely classical and his natural bent was for languages and literature, Henry decided to read mathematics. He was probably stimulated in this by a close and physically strongly-built friend from Truro, John Kempthorne, who was the son of an admiral and who had taken him under his wing as a frail young boy at primary school.

John Kempthorne had won a very high mathematical honour at Cambridge with a display of quite extraordinary diligence, and he inspired his junior to show the same purposeful determination. So it was that in spite of his lack of grasp of the fundamentals of Euclid, which at first led him to despair, Henry managed with perseverance and proper help to be successful in that field. He had the high honour of being proclaimed Senior Wrangler (meaning he graduated first among the honours students in his class) in January 1801, only five years after his friend and model, John, achieved the same. He was not yet 20. Then one year later he became a Fellow of St John's College where he won the first prize for a Latin essay, open to those who had just taken the Bachelor of Arts degree. Notwithstanding his capacity in the abstract science of calculations and formulae, his early love of the classics of Greece and Rome prevailed over his later mathematical studies to shape him into an avid and gifted philologist.

St. John's College, Cambridge – 'the pivot of destiny'

And yet earlier in his studies, in 1797, his father and younger sister, Sally, had known that all was not well with him. He was still only 16, and St John's was far away from his Christian home in Cornwall. While he may have been keen to please his ambitious father with his student merits, he was worried about a matter which had become very important to him. His spiritual understanding had not kept pace with his academic achievements, and he passed through a phase of great inward distress. Most regarded him as an amiable and quiet youth, and although he pretended to be irreligious he maintained high moral standards. Beneath that calm exterior there was a ferment of passionate emotions. His lack of peace only served to feed the flame of a hidden temper. There were moments when it burst out in a blaze of ugly passion. He had always been apt to break into sudden anger when his feelings were stirred beyond control. His worst offence was to fling a knife at a friend called Cotterill. He was shocked to see it stick and quiver in a wooden panel, and much relieved that, after all, the sharp object had not injured the student.

Happily, this young man who lacked self-control had been chosen by God in His absolute sovereignty (see Jn. 15:16; Eph. 1:4-7), just as the young tempestuous John, one of the two disciples surnamed by Jesus 'sons of thunder' (see Mk. 3:17; Lk. 9:52-55) was destined to be the so-called 'apostle of love.' The beardless Henry, still very boyish to look at, once touched and transformed by the power of God's grace, and growing in it (see 2 Pet. 3:18), became different in his disposition and started to show, if not perfectly, at least some elements of spiritual serenity and forbearance (see 2 Cor. 5:17; Phil. 4:13).

But that was still in the future. In the meantime, Henry's concerned relatives prayed for him and tried to help him spiritually by their letters. For all their efforts, he remained indifferent to their counsel if not arrogant at times toward his father. On holiday at home in 1799, he promised his younger sister Sally that he would start reading the Bible for himself. But once back in college, he found Isaac Newton's (1642-1727) theories far more congenial than the Holy Scriptures.¹ It needed more than Sally's loving persuasion to bring the self-opinionated undergraduate to his knees, but she was also praying for him. Afterwards he acknowledged that her intercession played a large part in his conversion as he went through an adolescent crisis and deep sorrowful loss. Later he bitterly regretted his lack of consideration: 'I do not remember a time in which the wickedness of my heart rose to a greater height than during my stay at home. The consummate selfishness and exquisite irritability of my mind were displayed in rage, malice and envy, in pride and vain glory and contempt of all; in the harshest language to my sister, and even to my father, if he happened to differ from my mind and will.' (Jesse Page, *Henry Martyn: pioneer missionary to India and Islam* p. 21.) So it was in his case, as in some others, that 'what the living could not do, the dead accomplished.'

Godly Influences

While still at college in January 1800, aged 19, Henry received the news of his father's sudden death. It came as a great shock and led him to seriously consider the gospel message. He wrote to his sister: 'After the death of our father, you know, I was extremely low-spirited, and, like most other people, began to consider very seriously, without any particular determination, that invisible world to which he was gone, and to which I must one day go.' John Kempthorne, his close friend from Truro, who was also a Christian, came to the bereaved young man to bring some consolation after vain attempts in the past to share the gospel with him. Now at his repeated suggestion, they read together helpful passages of Holy Scripture. Henry surrendered his life to the Lord Jesus as his Saviour and not long afterwards decided to study the Bible for himself, not only for comfort now but also as a guide for daily living. 'Little did John Kempthorne realise at this moment how important his advice was for his young friend, during this period of crisis and despair, which proved to be a catalyst for Henry's extraordinary service to God in future years' (John R C Martyn, *Henry Martyn (1781-1812), Scholar and Missionary to India and Persia: a Biography* p. 12). He let himself be drawn by Christ's offers of mercy and forgiveness, and began to pray with eagerness and hope. He had at last found a substitute for the father he had lost: a loving Saviour. His affectionate and devoted sister Sally, so full of zeal for the Wesleys' evangelical revival, could only rejoice that her clever brother had finally made a clear commitment to Christ the Lord.

Now a Christian and in his last years as an undergraduate student, Henry came under the godly influence of Charles Simeon (1759-1836) who had been Rector of Holy Trinity church since 1782. He was a keen evangelical and, as such, not always popular![2] Simeon was a gifted and indefatigable expositor of the Bible in that one congregation for 54 years, not wavering from the three-fold purpose of his preaching: 'to humble the sinner, to exalt the Saviour, to promote holiness' (Handley C G Moule, *Charles Simeon* p. 52)**.** Being a man of strong biblical convictions, he was satirised but he did not refrain from proclaiming unpopular truths such as the three crucifixions:

> *Christ crucified for me* – Gal. 3:1
> *The flesh crucified in me* – Gal. 5:24 & Rom. 6:6
> *The world crucified to me* – Gal. 6:14 & Col. 2:20.

Yet as time rolled by, more and more students attended his services. And some of these visited the domineering, yet gentle, considerate, affectionate and often quite humorous bachelor in private to discuss spiritual matters. Notable among them was Henry. Not only did the new Christian come to know the devout servant of God, but the whole tenor of his life was strikingly affected by the providential association. '… in Charles Simeon the sensitive orphaned student from Cornwall had found someone without whose love and support he could hardly have survived.' (Hugh Evan Hopkins, *Charles Simeon of Cambridge* p. 149.)

Charles Simeon (1759-1836)

Simeon, a preacher and shepherd, took a particular interest in each one of his flock and never ceased to lay before his young followers the importance of the ordained ministry. 'Students who came under Simeon's influence later became some of the great leaders of the Church both in Great Britain and around the world. His informal gatherings of undergraduates in his home for Bible study and prayer were perhaps the most influential part of his work. Scores of students first came to a personal relationship with Jesus Christ. Here they began to understand the Word of God and its implications for their lives. And here they received their first vision of reaching out to others with that Word' (David Howard, *Student Power in World Missions* in *Perspective on the World Christian Movement. A Reader* edited by R D Winter & S C Hawthorne: Pasadena, William Carey Library, 1981). Besides recommending young men to enter that ministry, however, he also had a vital interest in missionary work, especially in

India and the Far East. He knew how to whet the sense of purpose in one of his protégés (see 2 Tim. 2:1, 2), and Henry could not remain deaf to the appeals of this respected servant of God. During his holidays they pursued their fellowship by exchanging letters, and Simeon aroused in him a longing to walk with God in obedience and holiness. At first he had been inclined to reject the idea of Christian ministry, 'chiefly because he could not consent to be poor for Christ's sake,' as he said. He was thinking of studying law which was a promising career and offered the prospect of a lucrative job. But his view gradually changed and he turned his full attention to preparing himself for God's service.

As David Bentley-Taylor, one of his more recent biographers, has written: 'Henry's conviction and character were shaped by Simeon's teaching, till there grew up between them a warmth of affection and mutual admiration, which fortified Henry all his days. Born in a countryside deeply influenced by Wesley …, drawn to Christ through his father, Sally and Kempthorne, and then trained by Simeon, it was his destiny to carry the Gospel to lands Wesley and Simeon never saw and at a price God never asked them to pay' (David Bentley-Taylor, *My Love Must Wait; the Story of Henry Martyn* p. 16).

Charles Simeon was to remain the closest of Henry's Cambridge friends. It was through him too that he was to meet a fellow student from King's College, John Sargent (1780-1833), who, like Simeon, came from a wealthy family but found his true treasure in heaven. John became one of Henry's intimate friends to whom he confided his thoughts. He was probably the one person who understood the somewhat unpredictable Henry best of all, for though converted his natural characteristics were still part of his makeup. He was a man of intense emotions, moving quickly from rapturous joy to the sloughs of despair.

Among other acquaintances Henry made during his time at Cambridge was Henry Kirke White (1785-1806), who was from Nottingham. A deist, he enrolled at St. John's College in 1804, planning to become a minister, and was converted at around the

Henry Kirke White (1785-1806)

same age as Henry. The young, precocious and promising poet wrote, among other hymns, 'The Star of Bethlehem.' According to the opinion of Robert Southey (1774-1843), the promising boy-poet would have shone brightly in the firmament of literary stars had he continued to develop his skill. Frail and pale-faced, he also came into the sphere of fellowship of Simeon. He shared many of Henry's exercises, though he arrived at college when the other had already made up his mind to leave all behind him, was fully engaged in Christian ministry and about to leave for the foreign field. This may well have inspired or strengthened the newcomer's determination to enter into God's service himself. The two became fast friends and had much in common, but the junior was to precede the senior to the grave. He died at the age of 21, before he could graduate and without fulfilling his aspirations, five months after Henry's arrival at Calcutta, and of the same insidious tuberculosis that was to cut short Henry's life ten years later.

When just 21 and prompted by reading the *Life and Diary of David Brainerd* (1718-1747), the famous Puritan

*David Brainerd
(1718-1747)*

with the claims of Christ as Lord, and realising more and more that God had a specific plan for his life, there was a new consideration to take into account.

Back in Cambridge in April 1802, Henry had the honour of being accepted as a Fellow in one of England's most illustrious colleges. Although he was almost without a rival among the mathematicians at Cambridge, his real interest was in the classics, both literature and languages. Yet he was happy to help struggling students who would call in for explanations of mathematical problems. No doubt a brilliant academic career lay before him, but something else had been exercising a stronger inner pull in a different direction for some time. He may have heard John Wesley's motto ringing again and again in his ears: 'Saved to serve!' This propelled him into another vocation. He sought the perfect will of God alone and with his special friends, and he felt more and more drawn to something which became much more meaningful in the light of eternity:

to be a servant of the Lord to proclaim the gospel! (see Ps. 32:8, 33:18; Is. 30:21).

Decision and Opposition

Before the end of 1802, Henry had made his first approach to the newly founded (1799) Church Missionary Society (CMS) with a view to being sent out to India. The board of the embryonic society was extremely surprised to receive the candidature of one of Cambridge's most brilliant scholars. 'It was an age when the Church had hardly begun to think in terms of its missionary calling, but he offered himself as a missionary to the newly formed Society.' (Marcus Loane, *Henry Martyn: a Star in the Orient* in *They were pilgrims* p. 52.) Complying with the suggestion of Charles Simeon to become his curate, Henry was first accepted as a deacon (1803) while still involved in his academic studies and tutoring. Then after further reading in theology, he was finally ordained at the age of 24 as an Anglican minister at the Chapel Royal in St James's in London (1805).

It was easy for the scholarly young man to become an associate of Simeon, despite his false modesty in thinking that he lacked sufficient piety and proper preparation. The novice felt a lack of assertiveness and eloquence in his preaching when trying to match the passionate fluency of the Rector of Holy Trinity, but he knew that this training was necessary as he had made up his mind to become a missionary.

Both at Cambridge and in his home town, Henry's step to devote himself as a missionary in a distant exile was regarded as fantastic and absurd. He was burying his talents, they said, and wasting his gifts, when his scholarship and learning could be better used at home. Some colleagues felt betrayed by his leaving them and the university's corridors of glamorous prestige for a post of no significance in an obscure and primitive culture! Among his Christian friends some were not keen either on the idea of missionary work. Some appear to have been in the tradition of the hyper-Calvinists who accused William Carey (1761-1834), the determined English Baptist promoter of foreign missions, of enthusiasm for thinking that God needed his help in converting the heathen. Most serious was the objection of his young sister, Sally. She did not object to missionary work as such but felt that her brother was 'unqualified through want of religious experience,' and faithfully told him so. Besides, she was concerned for his delicate health which would not cope, in her opinion, with the strain demanded. But his calling was on firmer ground and could stand the tide of opposition and criticism. Above and beyond all the arguments, he gradually became convinced of the call of God to foreign missionary work, and despite his painful sense of unfitness and loneliness in his decision he never again seems to have thought of any other course of action. His life-long conviction of the sovereign wisdom and power of God lay at the back of this resolve: if it was God who called he could not refuse and the issue must be in God's hands. He was content to leave the matter there and rest in God's peace and promises.

Another man of great intellectual attainment and prominence, Saul of Tarsus who became the Apostle Paul, could declare without the slightest embarrassment: 'What things were gain to me, these I counted loss for Christ ... One thing I do, forgetting those things behind and reaching forward to those things which are ahead, I press toward the goal for the prize of the upward call of God in Christ Jesus' (Phil. 3:7, 13-14). What views had Henry of the necessity which he felt laid upon him to preach the gospel? His first conviction was the sinfulness and helplessness of all men in the sight of a just and holy God. Like many of the great missionaries of his day, he believed in God's election of His people not as a mere theological quibble but as an obvious fact of experience. And like them, he saw no inconsistency between this belief and a zeal to win people for God; indeed, far from being a barrier to evangelism, it provided the strongest of incentives to know that he was an instrument in the hands of the Almighty God.[3]

John Wesley (1703-1791)
For 55 years, John Wesley travelled tirelessly on horseback across Great Britain visiting both urban and rural areas with the gospel. His preaching and teaching, stirred by God's grace, contributed to a great spiritual awakening and led many to nothing short of full devotion to the Lord. He and his brother Charles, the well-known hymn writer, changed the face of 18th century England from a spiritual point of view.

As a young Christian, Henry may have heard and even sung the well-known hymn of Charles Wesley (1707-1788) that ignited the spark that fired many in the church to worldwide evangelism and gave such an impetus to the modern missionary movement:

> O for thousand tongues to sing
> My great Redeemer's praise.
> The glories of my God and King,
> The triumphs of His grace!

My gracious Master and my God,
Assist me to proclaim,
To spread through all the earth abroad
The honours of Thy name.

(Written in 1739)

Early in 1804 Henry's plans received a serious blow when he found that he had lost the inheritance left by his father for reasons beyond his control. This left him with his 22-year-old unmarried sister, Sally, entirely dependent on him. A missionary salary would not be sufficient for this. Confronted with this new situation, Simeon suggested that he apply to

Holy Trinity, Cambridge, in 1803
Henry served as a curate to Charles Simeon in this church.

be a chaplain to the East India Company. The post carried a large salary, and while its duties were primarily among the company's European employees, it might be expected to leave considerable scope for work among the natives. After some vacillation as he wondered about the fulfilment of his wish to be able to live simply and remain an independent missionary, he offered himself on Simeon's advice to the Company as a chaplain and was accepted in April 1805.[4] (And yet in such a position, according to a recent survey by the late Dr. Frederick A. Tatford, 'the chaplains associated with the Company were perhaps not the most acceptable recommendation to the Indian people, and the missionary work may have suffered somewhat in consequence of this. It certainly did from the attitude shown by the officials of the Company in later years' (Frederick A Tatford, *The Challenge of India* in *That the World May Know* p. 72).

The East India Company was a British enterprise founded in 1599, more interested in worldly trade profits than in the kingdom of God. It was known in the past to be opposed to the idea of proselytising and to missionaries going to other lands to seek to convert the heathen. But now the directors of the company, perhaps through the powerful influence of John Wesley and some leading Christian politicians such as William Wilberforce (1759-1833),[5] had been concerned for some time about the welfare of their employees across the seas. They realised the need for spiritual help and guidance for men serving in places far from their native land, and Charles Grant (1746-1823), Chairman of the Board of Directors in London from 1794, set about looking for dedicated men of evangelical faith to fill the position of chaplains in Bengal.[6] Against all the odds hindering a free course for the cause of Christ in the East, 'Grant and his associates worked to establish Christian missions in India with Government support and protection' (C H Philips, *The East India Company, 1784-1834* p.159). Fortunately the company was offering a substantial stipend for the job and this became a course Henry could take. He was also thrilled to hear that a fellow-student from Cambridge,

Daniel Corrie (1777-1837), was also presenting himself to serve the Lord in India, to be followed by another of Henry's close acquaintances, Thomas T. Thomason (1774-1829). They all became chaplains in Bengal by 1808 and all were protégés of Charles Simeon.

Vocation and Preparation

Henry had begun to keep a brief journal during 1802, but his published journals date from January 1803. They open a window into his heart and throw a wealth of light on his spiritual pilgrimage and insights. His great concern was to rule his heart by the perfect will of God, and his journal on 30 March 1803 refers to this: 'To keep the heart clean is a hard matter indeed, and what I know very little about; it requires more labour, care, self-denial than my flesh can easily submit to.' His pietistic consciousness of sin and uselessness was balanced by consecrated exertion (see 1 Cor. 9:25-27. The Apostle Paul exemplified what is personal discipline in this statement: a

Taj Mahal by W. Daniel, 1834[7]

sober look, a straight run, a solid fight, and he encourages us to follow in his footsteps – 1 Cor. 11:1, Phil. 3:17, 4:19). His journals were a private thing, not written for publication, but when his friends eventually opened them after his death they found an authentic record of the way in which this Christian had sought to discipline himself in his determination to lead a life of self-denial. It was a life modelled on David Brainerd in which he mortified himself in regard to every kind of worldly pleasure. It remains a treasure of great price for succeeding generations.

Henry's spiritual life did not stop at gratitude for the forgiveness of sins and salvation. We find in his writings increasing and deepening longings after the Lord, numerous instances of delight and satisfaction in fellowship, and many indications of his intense love for the Word of God. He was an early riser and his habit seems to have been to get into the lanes and fields at half-past five, preparing by meditation what he called 'right spirit and a happy frame' for the hours of the day. He disciplined himself early in prayer and fasting for the utmost service, and his cry was: 'If there be anything I do, if there be anything I leave undone, let me be perfect in prayer.' His relationship with Simeon was growing in mutual affection during his last years in England. The older man looked on him as a son, and he looked up to Simeon as a father. But he could not escape the price which such friendship entailed. His journal dated 22 April 1803 makes this clear, disclosing a lifelong inclination to disparage himself and tendency to dwell on his sinfulness: '… was ashamed to confess that I was to be Mr. Simeon's curate; a despicable fear of men from which I vainly thought myself free.' (Samuel Wilberforce, *Journals and Letters*, Vol. 1, p. 38.) And yet, surely Simeon's spiritual influence helped shape and colour the young man's life and path as they learned together a total dependence on the Lord. The long distance which was to separate them did not in any way alter the strong bonds of friendship despite the years of separation. And so a true and lasting friend is indeed a gift

The East India Company office, Leadenhall Street, London, by James Malton, late 18th century, demolished 1862
Although many places associated with the memory of Henry Martyn have disappeared, as for instance the magnificent building above, pulled down in 1862, the Chapel Royal of St. James (an integral part of St. James's Palace) still stands, where he had for a short time the office of a deacon while staying in London.

from God; a 'Jonathan' in pleasant and adverse circumstances, an intercessor (see 1 Sam. 19:4) and a supporter (see 1 Sam. 23:16).

There are two famous 19th century biographers of Henry Martyn. The first one, already mentioned, is John Sargent, a confidant of Henry's at Cambridge. They exhorted one another mutually in the ways of the Lord. In a letter dated 30 June 1803, we read: 'Dear Sargent ... May we be both conformed to the bright image of the Redeemer, especially in the meekness and lowliness of heart.' George Smith is the other writer who produced a voluminous and important biography, published in

The Chapel Royal

1892. Both narratives played a major role in perpetuating the memory of this missionary, prompting a present-day secular author, Avril Powell, to write, 'most accounts of Martyn's life and achievements have been hagiographical' (Avril Powell, *Muslims and missionaries in pre-Mutiny India* p. 89). Perhaps she wished for more insights on the social impact of his Christian undertaking on Indian society, something comparable to William Carey's endeavours. Among several popular and well researched biographies of the 20th century, the latest English one was produced by John R. Martyn (a distant relative of Henry's half-brother John). Meticulous, objective and free from sentimentalism, it was released in 1999.

In many of Henry's own writings, filled as they are with lengthy religious musings, one notices his pastoral inclination – his genuine concern for the welfare of those so dear to him and even more precious to the Lord. It may be that he learned from Simeon, his mentor, how to care and minister God's grace in receiving it himself to help those struggling with the problems and temptations of life (see 1 Cor. 11:1; Phil. 4:9; Gal. 6:1; Eph. 4:29; 2 Cor. 6:1). A sensitive person, he was easily moved and prone to tears in being exposed to the consequences of sin or in being told about the harrowing stories of the slave trade and other revolting injustices. Among other persons of interest, Henry had the privilege to meet and hear during his visits and short stay in London the aged preacher John Newton (1725-1807). His famous hymn '*Amazing Grace*' (written in 1779) tells of his dramatic conversion at the age of 23 from a background of debauchery as a sea-faring youth engaged in the slave-trade. After his conversion, he became a fierce opponent of the trade, no doubt to the delight of the young Henry.

The tall, slim, curly haired 22-year-old Henry struggled in vain with feelings of pride and self-importance at his ordination as a deacon at Ely Cathedral, 15 miles north-east of Cambridge, on 22 October 1803. At the same time he dreaded the 'weight and difficulty of the work that lay before me,' which never appeared so great at a distance! His air of confidence and good humour masked his confessed feelings of diffidence and sadness, and his debilitating self-doubts which often verged on despair. Walking back to his lodging in Cambridge that night he could 'scarcely believe that so sacred an office should be held by one who had such a heart within!' With such feelings he began his ministry as Simeon's curate and took charge of the neighbouring small parish of Lolworth. The same sentiments occur in his diary though they are generally happily combined with an acknowledgement of the faithfulness and goodness of the God who had placed this responsibility upon him.

In general Henry never saw much fruit from his work, except for some individuals but that did not alter the commission to preach, and it was this that did not let him rest. His diary often refers to the figure of the watchman in Ezekiel chapter three upon whom God lays the responsibility of the death of those he failed to warn. He had no doubt of the hopelessness and lost condition of those who die without Christ, and he was commissioned by God to witness to them before it was too late. He was grieved to find in his native Cornwall that his evangelistic zeal was perceived as an affront, if not a provocation, to the old rigid religious establishment. Even in the congregation where he had been baptised as an infant he was not welcomed to minister. Possibly his preaching was not characterised by an oratorical gift, but it is on record that he always spoke, whether in his native land or foreign parts, at the sea or on the shore, with solemn earnestness as 'a

Henry in the clerical garments he wore for his ordination
The origin of this print is not known for sure but it is thought to be from the Evangelical Magazine of 1823.

dying man to dying men.' And when complimented by a very few appreciative listeners of his sermons, he would not hesitate to add: 'Unless their hearts are pricked it would be better I had never preached!' While some preachers may have been satisfied to entertain their audiences, Henry only looked for transformation through his proclamation of the gospel.

[1] Twelve years afterwards, on a ship in the Indian Ocean, Henry Martyn wrote: 'I bless God for Sir Isaac Newton, who beginning with the things next to him, and humbly and quietly moving to the things next to them enlarged the boundaries of human knowledge more than the rest of the sons of men.' A philosopher and mathematician, Newton, like many scholars of the 17th and 18th centuries, was a Bible-believing Christian who did not see a dichotomy between the progress of true science and faith in God and His revelation, the Bible.

[2] This reformer of the 18th century Church of England endured ten years of severe persecution at the University of Cambridge where he was Rector at Holy Trinity church from 1782 to 1836. Parishioners locked their pews so that alternative seating had to be arranged, colleagues refused to speak to him and students persistently hooted at him. But ultimately his perseverance and endurance paid off, and many were blessed and enriched. (Countless have been the true servants of the Lord, admired, envied and reviled from biblical to modern times. See 1 Cor. 4:12-14. The past should never be disregarded but treasured! See James 5:10.) Charles Simeon was instrumental in the founding of both the Church Missionary Society (1799) and the British and Foreign Bible Society (1804), reflecting his interest in the propagation of the gospel in Great Britain and other countries. In him we see that a Christian may pursue a settled ministry in one particular place and yet have an influence on a much broader front. Early on at Cambridge, Henry made himself personally known to this devout servant of God. See Hopkins, H E *Charles Simeon of Cambridge*, London: Hodder and Stoughton, 1977.

[3] I recommend the excellent book *Evangelism and the Sovereignty of God* by J. I. Packer, London: Inter-Varsity Fellowship, 1961, to any reader interested in this subject. Many have struggled with and debated this apparent dichotomy or paradox down the centuries but I am reminded of what the well-known Baptist preacher Charles Spurgeon (1834-1892) said when asked if he thought the heathen who had never heard the gospel would be saved. He replied pertinently, 'It is more a question with me whether we, who have had the gospel and fail to give it to those who have it not, can be saved.'

[4] The East India Company was granted a charter by Queen Elizabeth 1 in 1600 conferring on it a commercial monopoly on trade with India. The company established bases in Madras (1640), Bombay (1661) and Calcutta (1690) among other places, and entered into fierce competition for control of the vast sub-continent with rival representatives of other countries like France. However, the expenses incurred in this, and mismanagement and abuses of corrupted officials, resulted in a critical financial situation. This obliged the company to seek help from the British government, which progressively took control of the enterprise, notably by means of the India Act of William Pitt (1784). The commercial monopoly of the company was abolished in 1813, and after the Indian Mutiny (1857) British India came directly under the authority of the Crown. This led to the apogee of colonial domination there which had good and bad consequences for the Christian cause. J Nehru (1889-1962) in *The Discovery of India* (1944) gave us his own assessment of the East India Company: 'The corruption, venality, nepotism, violence and greed of money

of these early generations of British rule in India ... is something which passes comprehension.' 'It was,' he added, 'significant that one of the Hindustani words which has become part of the English language is "lot."' For a more recent re-appraisal, no less critical, see Nick Robin's *Imperial Corporation: Reckoning with the East India Company.*

5 William Wilberforce, known as a forceful advocate of the abolition of slavery, also promoted the distribution of Bibles by creating a society for that purpose in 1803. This led the following year to the formation of the British and Foreign Bible Society of which he was a founder member and Vice President. He championed the cause of overseas missions and evangelisation, and 'devoutly believed that the people of the Sub-Continent must not be denied access to the one true faith.' (Cormack, Patrick *Wilberforce: the Nation's Conscience* p.120.)

6 Charles Grant served in India and rose te be a senior merchant and then a member of the Board of Trade at Calcutta, obtaining a large fortune. Friendship with Christian Frederic Schwartz, one of the Danish-Halle missionaries in Bengal, later led him to campaign for the promotion of Christianity and education in India. His son, Charles, born in Calcutta (1778), graduated at Cambridge the same year as Henry Martyn. It is possible that Charles introduced Henry to his father when he was in charge of the India House in London.

7 This majestic mausoleum – 'a monument of love' – was built between 1632 and 1654 at Agra, then the capital of the Mogul Empire, by order of Shah Jihan in memory of his beloved young spouse. India has the third largest Muslim population in the world, after Indonesia and Pakistan. Its 125 million Muslim citizens make up about 12% of the population.

2

THE COST OF TOTAL COMMITMENT

Miss Lydia Grenfell

For all Henry's determination to share the gospel with those outside his own country, there was a hindrance that could have kept him from moving ahead with his plan. This was a deep and sincere relationship with Lydia Grenfell (1775-1829), his cousin's sister-in-law, which began in the summer holidays of 1804 at Marazion in Cornwall. Henry had known Lydia from childhood, but was six years younger. It is possible that this and his own insecurity made him too shy to openly confess his feelings and propose to her at once. He came to realise that he had missed a perfect opportunity, but was comforted in his regret by Lydia's eldest married sister Emma, who was also a close friend, who told him that his affection was not unrequited. Then, several months later, when he and Lydia met again, he was more bold and told Lydia about his love. He asked her if she would join him in India if marriage there was recommended, but she refrained from responding to his offer. He wrote to Emma admitting that he loved Lydia more than ever although he was overcome by sadness.

Since her conversion in 1800 through an emotional crisis, Lydia had become a devout and active Christian. She worshipped at the local Methodist chapel in the ancient town of Marazion, and visited the poor and sick of the neighbourhood to bring practical help and read and pray with them. Her diary has much in common with Henry's: full of critical self-examination and revealing a longing for more holiness and fellowship with God.

The appearance of this lady, at the ripe age of 30, was overwhelming for Henry. It seemed to him, at least in the beginning, that his love for her and his vocation were deadly rivals. 'I devoted myself unreservedly to the service of the Lord,' he wrote in 1804, 'to Him, as the One who knew the great conflict within, and my firm resolve, through His grace, of being His, though it should be with much tribulation.'

A missionary call probably meant hardship and banishment for life, as he understood it. Supposing, he thought, she could love him, could he involve her in this? Then there was his uncertainty of earlier days about the wisdom of taking a life-partner to help fulfil his calling. As for Lydia, her

Marazion in Cornwall in the 18th century

domineering mother, Mary, with whom she still lived, proved reluctant to let her youngest daughter follow Henry in his undertaking. Perhaps she would have been less averse to Lydia marrying him had he refused to obey God's will and chosen a more comfortable family life in a parsonage in England. And, indeed, such a temptation crossed his mind.

Lydia, at 19, had become engaged to a solicitor from Penzance, Samuel John, but broke with him after nearly six years in the summer of 1800. She remained at home with her parents finding some solace in her new-found spirituality although far from happy in her pious introspection. Foolishly perhaps, she was unwilling to enter into another marriage contract while her ex-fiancé remained unmarried (he did

Mary Grenfell (1734-1826)
There is no existing picture of Lydia Grenfell.

The cost of total commitment

not marry until 1810). Had she been able to discuss this with Henry when they met, it is possible they would have both been spared much heartbreak. His diary and letters disclose his inner feelings and hope to marry her, but her indecisiveness became almost a mental torture to him.[8] It was his devotion to God that led him to obey and leave England for distant regions without her though she was not willing to follow, but the cost of this would later prove to be a permanent cause of turmoil in his mind.

The diary which Lydia kept for 25 years from 1801 proves that her heart was at length won by him, though too late for earthly union. The two journals record the ebb and flow of hope in their relationship with human pathos and enthralling interest. 'I felt too plainly that I love her passionately. The direct opposition of this to my devotedness to God in the missionary way excited no small tumult in my mind.' He struggled by every means to forget her, but it was a losing battle. 'In dreams her image returned, and I awoke in the night with my mind full of her.' (*Journals and Letters*, Vol. 1, p. 146.) He was able, to some extent, but temporarily, to give up Lydia, not without agony, seeing that his duty called him to a different path. Yet, with praises, he could say: 'God has not forsaken me but strengthened me in my determination to go forth.'

It is startling to find frequently in the beginning of his diary, side by side with expressions of his ardent love, a persistent idea that it is better not to be married as this allows for free and undistracted service to God (see 1 Cor. 7). It is not clear whether the single Charles Simeon had influenced him to think along these lines, for other young men he had shepherded did marry, such as John Sargent and Thomas Thomason. For their part the people waiting for Henry in Calcutta were ready to welcome him as a married chaplain, and he knew that his lucrative salary would have been more than enough to support a wife and enable them to settle together in a comfortable house in India with servants at their disposal. The long conflict with its fluctuations between the pros and cons involved seemed at last to have been resolved when he summed it all up on 8 July 1805: 'How much have I gone through the last two or three years to bring my mind to be willing to do the will of God when it should be revealed.'

Henry was appointed by God to work in India; that was his settled conviction and nothing could turn him back from it! Throughout his short life his attachment for Lydia never left him although it was marked by profound dejection. That was the cost and the pain he had to endure as a result of his personal choice to follow what he understood to be God's plan for his life. Many may not have been able to take such a decision, to renounce a legitimate love – but he did with settled conviction.

To his close friend from Cambridge, John Sargent, he wrote on 9 January 1804: 'My dear brother, in the midst of all the afflictions of the Gospel, and truly there are not few, we shall also be made partakers of its consolations. The contemplation of the eternal world is of necessity my chief happiness, and yours, I hope, by choice, for though this world demands your attention more than mine, you have learned to give it its right value.' John, who was married, and who opted to study law and stay in Sussex to take care of his parents' huge estate, later said of Henry: 'He went forth to preach the Gospel to the heathen, and it was his firm resolution to live and die amongst them. When he left England, he left it wholly for Christ's sake, and he left it for ever.'

Temple Gairdner (1873-1928), a missionary burdened for the Muslim world who worked for many years in Egypt, was undoubtedly inspired by his forerunner's total commitment. He wrote: 'He had laid down literally his fame, the one love of his life, his whole future and his whole earthly joy' (Temple Gairdner, *The Reproach of Islam* p. 241).

Though Henry and Lydia never saw each other again, that is not the end of the story. It would take a considerable volume to hold all the letters that passed between them, and the thoughts about each other with which their diaries abound. Both were

Souvenir

This ivory tea caddy was given to Lydia by Henry before he left Cornwall for India (it is exhibited in the Royal Cornwall Museum in Truro).

and continued to be truly in love. Neither was fully reconciled to their separation until Henry's death, and that death took place on a journey at the end of which he had hoped to claim her as his bride.

Farewell to the Dearest

Henry joined a fleet of the East India Company in Portsmouth on 16 July 1805. It was bound for India under the direction of Captain Byng, and he was chaplain to the British troops. On the harbour quay was a large crowd of friends who had come from Cambridge and London to bid him farewell. Led by the dignified Charles Simeon himself, they promised to fast and pray for a safe journey. Charles solemnly grasped Henry's hand in his own hands and raised them to his lips, and then calmly departed. The newly married Sargent[9] and some others went on board the *Union* with Henry, and gave him an exuberant goodbye which touched the traveller. Maybe not all had the presentiment 'that they should see his face no more' (Acts 20:38).

The normal time for the fleet to reach India from Portsmouth was between five and six months, but Henry was at sea for over nine due, as we shall see, to several incidents. The ship anchored on the way at Falmouth in Cornwall for three weeks, and Henry was able to make an unexpected and quick visit to Marazion by coach. This was an opportunity to be more candid and settle things with Lydia as well as leave her with a small gift as an expression and remembrance of something which was definitely more than friendship. It was then, just before he left for the ship and its departure from English waters, that Lydia admitted that she had no objection whatever to coming out to India as his wife, but thought that he had better go out a free man. This suggested to him that his freedom would not have to last much longer.

The same night the vessel left Falmouth behind, Lydia felt that her love for Henry was beyond recall. She wrote in her diary: 'Dear friend now gone to return no more.' But her final words would have certainly surprised him: 'It is now clearly understood between us that he is free to marry where he is going and shall often pray the Lord for him to find a suitable partner.' For Henry, the only suitable partner was Lydia. 'Thus parted these two pious hearts, he to bear away the tenderest memory on his outward way, she with devotion to pray for richest blessings to descend upon him' (*Henry Martyn: pioneer missionary to India and Islam* p. 51).

Henry had left his native land for one cogent reason: he would not be 'disobedient to the heavenly vision' (Acts 26:19). This was in great contrast to the epitaph of the unknown man of God mentioned in 1 Kings, chapter 13 (see verse 26) who lived in vain! Henry was determined to obey God's voice and fulfil His purpose for his life, but felt all the pangs of nostalgia during the first weeks at sea. He was homesick for Cornwall and Cambridge, and his heart ached with love for that special lady he had left behind. Was he after all convinced that he had to remain single to carry on God's work? There is a growing uncertainty about this in his written record as he penned his pleas for her to share his life.

It was the greatest calamity of his whole career that Lydia did not accompany him. George Smith wrote, reviewing his life: 'His humility is quite undoubted, unfeigned, profound, sincere. There seems, however, to have been a touch of natural melancholy and depression, which was increased by one of his greatest mistakes, the leaving England with his affections tied to Lydia Grenfell, whom he ought either not to have loved or else to have married and taken her with him. Such an ecstatic, warm creature as Henry Martyn could do nothing by halves.

St. Michael's Mount near Marazion, Cornwall, in the 18th century
This shows the Mount at full tide. It was possibly the last sight Henry had of his native land on a journey to the East from which he was never to return.

Separation was martyrdom to such a tender heart.' (G. Smith, *Henry Martyn: Saint and Scholar* p. 554.)

Cast on the ocean, with the shores of England disappearing from sight, Henry wrote in his journal: 'Would I go back ? Of course no! But how can I be supported? My faith fails. I find, by experience, I am weak as water. O my dear friends in England, when we spoke with exaltation of the mission to the heathen, what an imperfect idea did we form of the sufferings by which it must be accomplished!' Long before, as he contemplated missionary service, he was aware of the danger of being carried away by the 'romance' of the work. 'I find greater pleasure at the prospect of it; I am conscious however, of viewing things too much on the bright side, and think more readily of the happiness of seeing the desert rejoice and blossom as the rose than of pain, and fatigue, and crosses, and disappointments.' He paced the deck of the ship on the long voyage to India holding tight in his hand the beautiful and comforting gift from his Cambridge friends that Simeon had passed to him in unfeigned Christian affection: a silver compass. Alone, with his memories, he had convinced himself that he could now safely dwell with tender feelings on all that lay behind.

The trauma of leaving and the events leading up to it, combined with the loneliness he felt in his new situation, had obscured for some time the brighter side of his character. His highly-strung nature was tormented by the remembrance of all that he had loved and left while his merciless self-examination rebuked him for his lack of commitment and dedicated holiness. But although given to melancholy and self-criticism when alone, he always had gracious charm and was ready to show humour when with friends and sympathetic listeners.

On 4 December 1804, he had written in his journal: 'Dearest Lydia! Never will thou cease to be dear to me; still, the glory of God, and the salvation of immortal souls is an object for which I can part with thee.' His conquest of himself appeared to be complete then. But for all her goodness she was not built in the mould of heroic sacrifice and she could not bring herself

The cost of total commitment

to let him slip out of her life. She had refused his request for correspondence, but she began to write and her letters revived all the buried feelings. Letters from England were few and far between, and they brought him little comfort when they did come. But he never faltered; he was more than willing to bear the cross of celibacy in order to follow Jesus Christ – so he reasoned or tried to convince himself – undisturbed by marital responsibilities. The letters from England came from John Sargent and Charles Simeon, from his sister Sally and his cousin Emma, and from Lydia. Her letters sometimes lifted his heart to the stars and sometimes dashed his hopes to the ground. His love for her, a steady and growing devotion rather than a self-destructive flaming passion pervades his own journal during those years like the refrain of sad and sweet background melodies. He desired with all his heart to live for the Lord alone but felt intensely the cost of this in terms of personal sacrifice.

Separation without Detachment

The first in a series of nine letters was lost at sea, but her next letter was placed in his hands at Calcutta on 12 July 1806. What true lover would not have been filled with hope when he read that she had him in her mind many times each day as she came before the throne of grace in prayer? 'You said in your letter,' he replied, 'that frequently every day you remember my worthless name before the throne of grace. This instance of extraordinary and undeserved kindness draws my heart toward you with a tenderness which I cannot describe. Dearest Lydia, in the sweet and fond expectation of your being given to me by God and of the happiness which I humbly hope you yourself might enjoy here, I find a pleasure in breathing out my assurance of ardent love. I have now long loved you most affectionately, and my attachment is more strong, more pure, more heavenly, because I see in you the image of Jesus Christ. I unwillingly conclude by bidding my beloved Lydia – Adieu.'

He posted a copy of this letter on 1 September 1806 with

a second letter in which he wrote: 'Now my dearest Lydia, I cannot say what I feel ... I could not if you were here: but I pray that you may love me, if it be the will of God, and I pray that God may make you more and more His child, and give me more love for all that is godlike and holy .... How earnestly do I long for your arrival. Though it may prove at last no more than a waking dream that I ever expected to receive you in India, the hope is too pleasing not to be cherished till I am forbidden any longer to hope. Till I am assured of the contrary, I shall find a pleasure in addressing you as my own. If you are not to be mine you will pardon me, but my expectations are greatly encouraged by the words you used when we parted in England, that I had better go out free, implying, as I thought, that you would not be unwilling to follow me if I should see it to be the will of God to make the request. It was rejoicing also to see your letter that you unite your name with mine when you pray that God would keep us in the path of duty; from this I infer that you are by no means determined to remain separated from me. You will not suppose, my dear Lydia, that I mean these little things to influence your conduct, or to implicate you in an engagement. No, I acknowledge that you are perfectly free, and I have no doubt that you will act as the love and wisdom of our God shall direct.'

Twelve months were to ensue in which his own supreme joy was to think of her and hope for an early matrimonial union. He was cheered by news from her in three more letters which have not been preserved, but which were all written before she received his invitation. The third in the series of nine was given to him on 24 September 1806, and he read a meaning between its lines which she had not perhaps meant it to bear. He was thankful to read that his name was still linked with her prayers; it made him feel that she was less aloof than she would have him think. He wrote: 'The Lord gave me near and close and sweet communion with Him on this subject, and enabled me to commit the affair with comfort in His hands. Why did I doubt His love? Does He not love us far better than

The cost of total commitment

Mystery!
This medallion of Henry Martyn, set in brass in a velvet case, is owned by Ridley Hall in Cambridge. At the back of the portrait is a plaited lock of blond hair. It may also be the miniature which had been made on 8th July 1805 for his sister Sally before Henry left England.

we love one another?' The fifth letter came on 3 July 1807, and so quickened all his feelings that he could think of nothing else. He now believed that he had won her heart, and hoped soon to win her hand as well.

Lydia's diary reveals more of her heart than her letters dared to disclose, for it sets down before God her loving concern on his behalf since the fleet had sailed from Europe. On 4 August 1806 she observed: 'One year is nearly passed since we parted, but scarcely a waking hour I believe he has been absent from my mind.'

It was on 2 March 1807 that she received his first invitation to go out and join him. Her mind was thrown into turmoil, but her private scruples and the interference of her mother kept her from accepting it. Therefore she wrote in her mother's name to refuse, and sought relief for her trampled feelings through her journal: 'Just two years since I parted from a dear friend and brother, whose memory will ever be cherished by me.' But her letter reached him at length on 24 October 1807, leaving him feeling as though his heart would burst with grief and disappointment. Lydia had not concealed her real wish, and her letter still left some room for hope. He saw the one loophole, and he sat down that night to plead his suit once more. 'You say that present circumstances seem to you to forbid my indulging expectations,' he wrote, 'as this leaves an opening, I presume to address you again, and until the answer arrives, must undergo another eighteen months of torturing suspense ... In the meantime, since I am forbidden to hope for the immediate pleasure of seeing you, my next request is for a mutual engagement ... The more I write, and the more I think of you, the more my affection warms ... Farewell, dearest, most beloved Lydia.'

8   There are a number of factors which may explain her reservation and her mother's objections. Some kind of misconduct, possibly in her courting relationship with Samuel John, may have held her back from the repeated advances of Henry Martyn. We can infer this from some of her notes showing a conscience troubled by a past moral lapse, and consequently seeing herself as unworthy of being united with him. However, she was worried at the same time that Henry would be wedded to someone else such as Daniel Corrie's sister who had joined her brother in India. It is also very likely that her mother, besides her excuses referred to already, was opposed to giving up her unmarried daughter, a companion and convenient nurse for herself in old age (she lived to the ripe old age of 92, dying only three years before her daughter). There is also a suggestion that differing social status, an important consideration in those days, made Henry incompatible for Lydia and the idea of marriage to him distasteful in the eyes of her mother. Whether Henry was aware of these factors or not, he was kept hostage by an illusory dream of Lydia's conscious or unconscious making. She seems to have found it difficult to accept his love openly and yet was not ready to refuse it.
9   He and his wife, born Mary Smith, named their son, who died in 1836 before coming of age, Henry Martyn Sargent.

3
THAT ALL MAY KNOW AND BELIEVE

Sea Voyage to India

Let us now go back and see what happened on Henry's journey after he bade good-bye to England on 16 July 1805. Though still a relatively young convert and something of a novice – his experience of ministry was limited to his brief time with the villagers of Lolworth and occasional sermons to his fellow students in Cambridge – the 24-year-old was put in charge of the spiritual welfare of a British regiment and Indian crew. He was the only chaplain in a force of 8,000 soldiers, some with their families, on what would prove an adventurous and uncertain voyage of nine months, including disease and near-shipwreck on treacherous reefs. Travelling by sea was also dangerous at this time because of the Napoleonic Wars (May 1803 to June 1815). It was not until October 1805 that the French/Spanish fleet threatening England was finally defeated by Horatio Nelson's victory at Trafalgar (off Cadiz in south west Spain). His ship, the *Union*, sailed via Cork in Ireland, the island of Madeira, Salvador in Brazil and the Cape of Good Hope, and reached Calcutta at the beginning of May 1806.

The *Union* was in convoy with many other commercial and military vessels. As they crossed the equator, an attack of dysentery swept through the ship. Henry spent many hours by the bunks of the sick, until he fell sick as well but fortunately only for a short time. Once recovered, he returned to his pastoral duties among soldiers and civilians, and beside the hammocks of the dying including the ship's captain. Among other incidents which made the journey difficult and prolonged was the battle of Blaauberg, near the Cape. As the fleet reached the south of Africa on 8 January 1806, 7,000 soldiers were ordered into battle by General Sir David Baird (1757-1829). They were given the task of defeating the Dutch presence in the Cape,

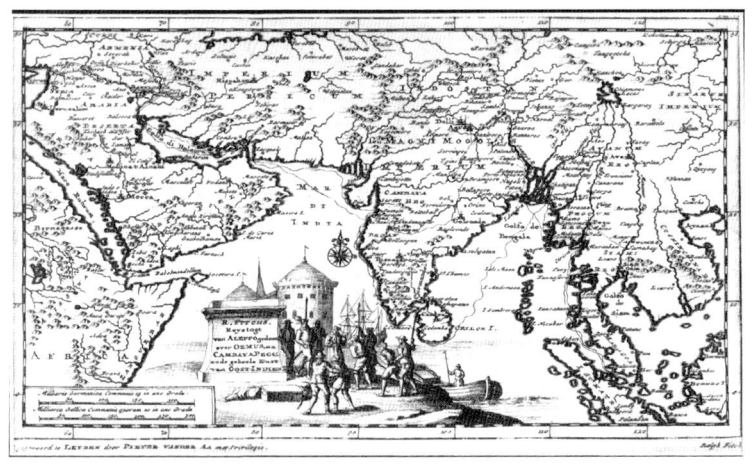

Map by Pieter van der Aa, 1707
From the 16th century for about 300 years, the European 'Christian' nations fought each other in a bitter contest for colonial expansion that had little to do with evangelising the peoples of the lands they conquered. This map includes an illustration of an incident in the lengthy conflict between the Dutch and the English.

which at that time was part of the Batavian Republic[10], an ally of France and regarded as a threat to the safety of British access to India. The ensuing British victory left many casualties, and Henry was disturbed by the arrogant boasting of the victors. He fell to his knees praying that England might cease from being so ungodly at home and rather encourage missionaries to spread the gospel of peace and love in these distant regions. Although a military chaplain, he was distressed and saddened at the bloodshed which was regarded as warlike glory then, more so than it is today. He recorded in his diary: '… I could find it more agreeable to my own feelings to go and weep with the relatives of the men whom the English have killed, than to rejoice at the laurels they have won.'

During his month-long stay on the Cape, he found some encouragement by meeting a veteran Dutch missionary, Dr.

Johan T. van der Kemp (1747-1811), of the London Missionary Society. He also introduced him to some of his colleagues and together they told him about their great success among the heathen. Henry listened avidly to their experiences in the field and could not help hearing in their stories reminders of what he had read in David Brainerd's writings. He looked forward with great expectation and excitement to finally reaching his own field of labour.

The fleet set sail again on 9 February, shortly before Henry's 25th birthday, but the passengers, wearied by the long journey to the Cape, felt gloomy at the thought of the long voyage to India. Not long afterwards, they were hit by a storm and seasickness, and then the dysentery reappeared, more extensively than before. Henry had to commit many young bodies to the deep, including one of the few pious men among the soldiers. With the trade-winds behind it the fleet made good progress, but the chaplain suffered from headache, dysentery, breathlessness and nervous irritability. He gave himself to ministry among the passengers and crew, several of them with families, but his inability to win over the officers and their cadets to his passionate evangelistic message was hard to bear. Most of the rough sailors and rowdy soldiers regarded the cleric in his black silk coat as an object of ridicule from the start to the end of the journey. Like much of his work for the Lord during his life it was hard service and he had to show great forbearance. He found himself too academic to get on well with some of the types on board, and may have realised that his sermons were too complex for most of his audience. He felt inadequate and out of his element. He was afraid and, worst of all, felt lonely and isolated from like-minded friends. He had never known such loneliness before. He admitted: 'I was more tried by the fear of men than I ever have been since God called me to the ministry. The threats and oppositions of those men made me unwilling to set before them the truths which they hated, yet I had no hesitation about doing it' (see Prov. 29:25; Gal. 1:10).

And so it was that his presence on the ship and his

Johan T van der Kemp (1747-1811)

Henry may have been apprehensive about what lay ahead in fulfilling his calling to India, but he found fresh encouragement from meeting this elderly pioneer who gave him a present of a valuable New Testament in Syriac as a remembrance of his visit, a precious present which would prove useful to him in time to come. We do not know whether he was aware or not of the young missionary's future task as a translator. Was it sheer coincidence that this book should be offered to him, or providence?

uncompromising stand had its impact. Although many were offended by his straightforward warnings of judgement and calls for repentance, there were a few who decided to follow Christ whatever the cost. While some turned away and scorned his preaching, there were others among the young soldiers who came to his cabin in private to talk with him. Pricked in their conscience under the obvious conviction of the Holy Spirit, some were in tears from being directly confronted with the demands of God and the claims of Christ. 'Martyn always preached expecting God to work and … He did' (Vivienne Stacey, *Life of Henry Martyn* p. 35).

Opposition and problems never caused Henry to despair of anything but himself, and only increased his trustful dependence on the Spirit of God. He fed his soul on the Word of God as he tried to feed others, and he poured out his heart in prayer with an intensified ardour. 'Blessed Jesus,' he wrote on 5 February 1806, 'Thou art all I want – a forerunner to me in all I ever shall go through as a Christian, a minister, or a missionary.' The diary is still full of times of delight in the love of God and longing for more of His presence. He was confident that he was doing what God wanted him to do, and he would choose nothing else despite all the hardship and ridicule. 'I am so far from regretting,' he wrote at the end of 1805, 'that I ever came on this delightful work. I could scarcely find a situation more agreeable to my taste. On, therefore, let me go, and persevere steadily in the blessed undertaking, through the grace of God dying daily to the opinion of men, and aiming, with a more single eye, at the glory of the everlasting God.'

After two more terrible months at sea, the island of Ceylon (Sri Lanka) came into sight and soon the ship turned north, entering the Bay of Bengal and anchoring for a few days at Madras, before continuing to its final destination at Calcutta. His experience of ministry on ship had certainly not been very encouraging. The rude treatment which he had received from both crew and passengers did not abate when he gave them a few words of earnest farewell at parting. His solemnity was satirised, and his deep yearning for their souls seemed ill-spent on hard and impenitent hearts. 'Yet,' he said, 'I desire to take the ridicule of men with all meekness and charity, looking forward to another for approbation and rewards.' His life was guided by the maxim: 'To believe, to suffer, to hope.'

Arrival at Calcutta

Though exhausted, Henry was relieved to reach his destination after so many difficulties and delays, and soon forgot the epic sea journey necessary to reach his field of labour. Calcutta was one of northern India's two Hindu centres along with Benares, just as Lucknow and Delhi were its two Muslim citadels (for the Sunni and Shia branches of the religion). Two days after his arrival on 16 May 1806, he wrote the words by which he is so much remembered: 'Now let me burn out for God!'[11] From that time until the end of his days, his life was consumed by a constant sacrifice to God and His service.

Henry had two predecessors as evangelical chaplains and missionary philanthropists: the Yorkshireman, David Brown (1763-1812), and the Scot, Claudius Buchanan (1766-1815), with whom at once he felt at ease in a common bond of Christian fellowship. From Calcutta, he was rowed with the tide 16 miles up the River Hooghly to Aldeen in an hour and a half. This was the country house of David Brown in the suburb of Serampore, which became Henry's residence in Lower Bengal.

Soon after his arrival which was at the height of the hot season, Henry suffered acutely from high fever. He was so cast down by this that he started to think that he would die with his work undone. He happily recovered from this serious attack, and becoming acclimatised began to find room for thankfulness in the exotic atmosphere of his adopted land. In due time, he paid a visit to Serampore to meet William Carey, the famous Baptist missionary who had been in the field for thirteen years already. It was his mission reports, read in the chapel at Cambridge, that had so definitely directed Henry's thoughts to India[12]. They were two men from different backgrounds but alike in their reading interests and evangelical fire, and with a common concern for the furtherance of the gospel. Yes, 'Now let me burn out for God!' were Henry's words and, even more, his motto. Not only was his heart aflame for the rescuing of the lost, it was on fire for God (see Ps. 104:4). He loved the Lord Jesus Christ, and

Claudius Buchanan (1766-1815)
Claudius Buchanan was a strong advocate for the spread of the gospel in the East both during and after his eleven-year residence in India. He returned to Great Britain in 1808 and contributed to the 1813 parliamentary debate over the allowance of missionary outreach in India apart from the East India Company's control.

because he loved Him he served Him. Is it not true that genuine commitment to the King of kings begins first with enraptured adoration of Him? Our first duty is to worship our Creator and Redeemer with a heart bursting with thanksgiving and praise, and then help to bring others into this privilege too. That was Henry's exercise and goal.

Henry was in a climate where he could do little to bring the thermometer much below 45 degrees Celsius (113° Fahrenheit). His inherited tuberculosis began to tell more and more, and once at least brought him within a hair's breadth of death. He

**Calcutta with Fort William in the foreground,
in the early 19th century**
This massive structure with its college opened in April 1800. It was in proportion to British involvement in India at the time and subsequent domination of the whole of the country. Several chaplains and missionaries were employed at the college which gained fame through some of its graduates who became outstanding imperial civil servants.

was surrounded variously by suspicion, hostility and apathy. There was remarkably little visible success to encourage him in Calcutta just as in other places where he laboured. But though he had never been very robust he pressed on, confiding his insights to his diary, and showing an unconquerable delight and trust in the Lord, and a genuine satisfaction with whatever the Lord saw fit to appoint (see 1 Tim. 6:6; Phi. 4:11).

The example of his saintly life, and his attitude and approach to the Muslims, proved to be the best testimony to the truth he preached. However much men differed from him and his opinions and methods, they respected him and knew him to be what Persians afterwards called him: 'Mard-o-Khuda,' a man of God. The simplicity of his walk carried a glorious aura imparted by divine grace alone, so much so that even his foes could not help being impressed and commenting upon it.

It cannot be denied there were occasions when he might have been censured for denigrating Islam as, for instance, a letter dated 8 February 1808 in which he referred to it as a 'filthy religion.' Was it the case at the beginning of his missionary service that ignorance prejudiced him against it? This may well be so as later we find him, especially in Persia, more tactful in his approach to Muslims and cautious in his criticism of their religion. An obvious process of learning through knowledge and experiences shaped his attitude and methods in his set purpose to testify to them about the gospel.

Among threats, abuses, and disdain, he persevered, calm, unwavering and fearless. He was always eager to testify to the reality of the Christian faith, and absorbed in the service of the Lord. He seemed to grow more and more critical of himself, but at the same time more confident in the One whose service was his purpose. He was none too strong physically, and although he impressed those who met him with his peaceful radiance and childlike happiness, particularly in times of relaxation, he was stern with himself. He lived with ascetic simplicity, but without taking this to extremes. He had found an ideal in Francis Xavier (1506-1552) in this connection.[13]

At the beginning, Henry stayed with David Brown, the veteran East India Company's chaplain and his wife and several children in Aldeen, outside Calcutta. Brown, another of Charles Simeon's associates, was a Hebrew scholar who encouraged Bible translation into many oriental languages. He was the first Provost of Fort William College, an institution established for the purpose of teaching English people the languages and customs of India. The newcomer settled down to help in the work of the local church while waiting for his assignment. He and Brown became close friends, having much in common; Henry's obvious pleasure at sharing in the other's family life was undoubtedly a reflection of his inner longing to have a family of his own. The thought of Lydia persisted in his mind, and eventually he discussed the whole matter with Brown, asking him to read one of her letters. The older man was convinced that the lady was waiting to be won over and he advised Henry to send a suitable reply to which reference has been made already.

On 2 March 1807, Lydia received Henry's first letter inviting her to join him in India. Despite her desire to be united with the man she loved, she felt obliged to decline this offer. 'The pain of writing to him is over,' she noted in her diary on 8 March, 'and I feel satisfied I wrote what duty required of me … Return, O my soul, to thy rest!' Little did she know how small her pain was when compared with the agonising heartache it caused Henry; how little rest it gave his soul. Her reply reached him on 24 October, and its contents filled his heart with grief. To his dismay he read that she was not coming out to him in India. Her letter was long and obscure giving as her only reason the fact that her mother would not give her consent. Henry marked that date as the most unhappy of his life as she crushed all his hope. Whatever may have been the feelings and recommendation of Charles Simeon in regard to this relationship at its beginning, he had come to see Lydia as an ideal partner for the young man he cared for. He had called on her as he knew about the matter and was informed that she had sent her answer to Calcutta some weeks earlier.

Their conversation and his appeal to her to join Henry were fruitless, and it was with a heavy spirit that he let his young friend know. The merit and necessity of marriage for the lonely and somewhat impractical Henry became very evident to him as it has been to some of his close friends while he was still in England. They now all felt that it was the magnet of true love rather than infatuation that attracted Henry and Lydia to each other. But she was now concerned that she had given Henry too much hope, and felt guilty that

Aldeen

David Brown and his family lived at Aldeen a few miles from Calcutta on the banks of the Hooghly. There was an ancient pagoda in the garden, originally devoted to Hindu idolatries. At the invitation of his host, Henry took up his abode in this large and imposing temple structure. To his mind it was very evocative, and as he sat there, preparing his sermons or singing praises and adoration to the Lord Jesus, he rejoiced 'that the place where false gods were worshipped was now become a Christian oratory.'

she had appeared to promise to marry him and then had not been free to do so.

When Henry wrote from his posting at Dinapore to tell David Brown the news, his words showed some of the heartache that he hid from others. 'It is as I feared. She refuses to come because her mother will not give her consent. Sir, you must not wonder at my pale look when I receive so many hard blows on my heart …' 'I cannot bear to part with Lydia,' he wrote, 'and she seems more necessary to me than life; yet her letter was to bid me a last farewell ... With Thee, O my God, there is no disappointment; I shall never have to regret that I love Thee too well.' In January 1808 he wrote to Charles Simeon to tell him that all hope of being joined to Lydia was at an end. 'I can not doubt any longer what is the Divine will, and I bow to it ... I never loved, nor ever shall love human creature as I love her.' But he made his second appeal to her to come to India to join him. Her reply, which did not arrive until 14 December, only renewed his pain. 'Prayer was my only relief,' he wrote, 'and, I did find peace by casting my care on God.' Her last letter came on Christmas Day in 1809, and he briefly remarked: 'Now everything is over!' This ended for a while the correspondence in which he had poured out all his love with exquisite tenderness. But he could not hide the pangs of a deeply wounded spirit, infused as it was at times by a passing bitterness. And yet, even as he was suffering the loss of so much of the world's joy and compensation, his devotion to Christ the Lord remained as strong as an iron anchor, the guiding principle in every part of his life.

Acquaintance with William Carey

Soon after his arrival in India, Henry had been told about William Carey's plan for the translation of the Scriptures into many languages, not yet knowing his own vital part in the ambitious project to bring the good news to Muslims. He was to spend some of his time at Serampore with Carey and his team, and together enjoy full Christian fellowship despite their doctrinal differences (see Eph. 4:1-3). He taught New Testament Greek to the young missionaries there and even joined them on their preaching tours in the delta region of Bengal. During his stay, the young Anglican clergyman must have been interested and stimulated by what he himself came to see more and more clearly to be the most vital means to reach the natives: the Word of God in their own everyday languages. With this view and goal, the central role and authority of the Bible was reasserted! And as the opportunity came, Henry threw himself with enthusiasm into the projects of his Baptist friends for the translation of Scripture. But there was a difference: they were all self-taught men whereas Henry had graduated at Cambridge and had profited from the best philological training that day could supply. He was at times rather sharply critical of the older men, and set himself a standard of scholarship which was beyond their reach.

In Bengal, the only chaplain who fully appreciated Henry's longing to reach out to the Indians and live among them rather than in the company of Europeans was Claudius Buchanan. He realised that to prevent him from doing so would break his heart. Henry chose for his temporary home an island where there was a mainly Indian population, unlike the foreign merchant city of Calcutta. Although burdened to witness to the natives, he was at times intolerant of some aspects of their culture and traditions, which he denounced with disgust as barbaric. These included the Suttee funeral rites in which the widow burnt herself on the pyre of her deceased husband. This was a common practice among Hindus, which the British colonial administration outlawed in 1829. Hindu idolatry was an ever-present source of pain to him and, just as the Apostle Paul's spirit was provoked within him when he saw that Athens was given over to idols (see Acts 17:16), so Henry was vexed by the grotesque idols to which worshippers offered sacrifices of flowers and even food. 'His soul was filled with the zeal of the Old Testament prophets against idolatry' (*Henry Martyn: Saint and Scholar* p. 143). The pious religiosity of the Muslims may have been less alien to him, and yet he was well aware of the differences between Christianity and Islam especially in regard to basic doctrines.

As a chaplain, Henry was not a completely free agent and his first duty was to the staff of the East India Company; he knew he must wait to hear where his posting would be. When still in Calcutta in 1806, he heard that his old friend from Cambridge

William Carey (1761-1834)
A most ordinary man with extraordinary capacities. William Carey became the so-called 'Father of Modern Missions.' He accomplished all with credit and thankfulness to God. His was a monumental work, acknowledged even by India's secular government which commemorated the bicentennial of his birth in 1961 with a stamp.

days, Daniel Corrie, had arrived. He too had come out to take up work as a chaplain, and there were lively scenes of joy when the two friends met (see 2 Cor. 7:6). All that Charles Simeon and John Sargent had been to him in Cambridge, David Brown and Daniel Corrie were to him in India. Brown was to spend 25 years in Calcutta from 1787 till his passing away in 1812, and Corrie served in India for 31 years, becoming the first Anglican bishop of Madras in 1835 until his death in 1837 at the age of 59.

Henry's earnestness as a chaplain was such that his friends in Calcutta and the Baptists in Serampore constantly pressed him to become the minister of the mission of the Old Church (the Anglican meeting place for the expatriate community) with all the advantages that would follow from this. But he declined such an offer, though it would be repeated, to direct his attention to reaching the natives, saying that 'the evangelisation of India is a more important object than preaching to the European inhabitants of Calcutta.' After five months of waiting there, he received his first appointment to a military station.

Assignment to Dinapore

Understandably, David Brown was very happy to have another chaplain with Henry's character and high qualifications with him, and no doubt would have gladly retained him in Calcutta. However, on 13 September 1806 Henry was appointed chaplain at Dinapore with its garrison and Bankipore with its civil service. Bankipore included the European suburbs of Patna (capital of today's Bihar State), which stretched along the Ganges river. For the next two and a half years this would be his parish, right in the middle of Indian Bengal. As we will see, his experiences there were not unlike those at Calcutta where the Europeans held aloof, the natives were shy and suspicious, and the work was generally uphill and difficult. His services were sometimes not attended by a single European, yet he was thrilled and thankful to get at least a few natives to hear him

Daniel Corrie (1777-1831)
Daniel Corrie was appointed chaplain in Bengal in 1806. His close relationship with Henry was a precious consolation in the midst of the frustrations and afflictions he encountered in India. Corrie shared the same missionary vision and burden of his close friend, and laboured for the rest of his life on the field.

explain the Word of God in their language, and bring together small groups of his own compatriots who were genuinely interested and involved in the things of the Lord.

    The journey from Calcutta to Dinapore was a slow one. It took six weeks for the barge Henry was on to be towed upriver against the current. He redeemed the time by improving his knowledge of some languages which he had partly studied in England. There, in addition to his clerical duties as curate, which he had taken very seriously, he had made time to investigate oriental languages and also undertake several lessons in Urdu given by John B Gilchrist (1759-1841),[14] who had recently resigned his post with the East India Company. Among Henry's favourite books were some of Gilchrist's grammars and bilingual dictionaries, tools which proved of great value in India and Persia. He also got to know some oriental literary works, and developed a liking for Persian literature, particularly the writings of such famous mystic poets as Saadi (1193-1290) and Hafiz (1320-1389). Did he sense then that he would become instrumental in translating the New Testament into a language he came to love so well? He had left his native land proficient already in Hebrew, Greek and Latin, and he read the Scripture in these languages and French with eagerness. Now he used his

River taxis and other shipping on the Hooghly
A postcard from the 19th century showing river craft similar to those Henry used. These stopped at different stations for short and long periods to leave and take on passengers. These houseboats were called budgerows.

spare time and brilliant linguistic gifts to study other languages with the set purpose of mastering some of them, though he did not yet know the contribution he would make in bringing God's Word to people in their own languages so that they might know and believe who Christ is and what He has done (see Jn. 20:30, 31; 1 Jn. 3:18, 5:20). Within a few months of his arrival in India, Henry had mastered Urdu with its roots in Persian and Arabic on the one hand and Sanskrit on the other. It was an impressive achievement. He was a genius in the linguistic field.

As usual his days were spent in the most assiduous industry, carefully perfecting his linguistic knowledge with some meticulous translation work. These studies, undertaken in surroundings that were not conducive to such an exercise, were very exhausting. It took a great deal of commitment and discipline for a man of his physical weakness to go on day after day with such an endeavour. His work, as he made his way up the Ganges, appears to have been equally divided between studies of languages on board the barge and tract distribution on the shore. It was his practice to rise early in the morning while it was still cool, land at the nearest point, and walk along the bank and through the villages, speaking to the natives and distributing Christian literature wherever they would accept it. He proved to be not only an academic but also an evangelist.

Henry was an enigmatic figure to most of the foreign troops in Dinapore. At first many resented him, but gradually he was appreciated, especially in the hospital where he found his main field of work among Europeans. Here, as elsewhere, he found the same response from Europeans: a scornful rejection of his message by the vast majority. Those who showed some slight interest in the gospel preaching often succumbed to pressure from their peers who sneered at them. Yet there were a handful who, often in secret, came to hear more of the gospel at his humble house situated in the military barracks. In time, 30 or so were gathering there most evenings for prayer and hymn-singing and lively Bible studies. It is reported that Henry had a fine voice and could sing many hymns by heart to the delight of those who had the privilege to hear him informally or in organised gatherings. Happily for him, he found with Major Young and his wife a Christian home where he was regularly invited to dine and enjoy Christian fellowship.

Although appointed to work among Europeans, it would have been a bitter disappointment if he had not been able to do something for the natives around him. After all he wanted to be a missionary! Dinapore was near Patna, the home of fanatical puritans of Islam. He was amazed by the need of the people: 'Reached Patna this afternoon. Walked about this scene of my future ministry with a spirit almost overwhelmed at the sight of the immense multitude.' He was deeply stirred not only by the great number of people but also by the spiritual darkness spread before his eyes. 'What a wretched life shall I lead,' he wrote on 23 November 1806, 'if I do not exert myself from morning till evening in a place where through whole territories I seem to be the only light' (John Sargent, *A memoir of the Rev Henry Martyn* p. 209). He was ever conscious of the tread of Christless feet on the wide path to eternal damnation. It was clear to him that these people 'were without Christ, being aliens from the commonwealth of Israel and strangers from the covenants of promises, having no hope and without God in the world' (Eph. 2:12). So he embraced every opportunity to witness to the mercy of God manifested through Jesus Christ (see Eph. 2:13-19), finding the language of the Bihar region different from Bengal, though Hindi is very close to Urdu in its spoken form. He was not deterred by opposition to his ministry among the native people on the ground that it was waste of time. There were other occasions during his career when he had to cope with murmuring (see Lk. 15:1, 2) and whispering (see Prov. 16:28; 2 Cor. 12:20) against his actions, even to the extent of malicious gossip designed to cast doubt on the transparency and integrity of his life. He knew that little could be done to avoid such attacks and the damage they can cause, and that his only recourse was to commit his cause to the Lord as exhorted in 1 Peter 5:6-9.

As Henry conversed with Hindus and Muslims, he felt more than ever before the importance of translating the Scriptures into their own tongues and even giving them an opportunity to be educated. His large salary and Spartan life-style meant that he had saved a considerable amount of money, which he used partly for the education of the natives in Dinapore and later in Cawnpore. He set up free schools, selecting teachers for them himself; a venture which had encouraging results but was not always appreciated by all. Nevertheless, the native population had a strong and loyal friend in Henry who was grieved when he saw the oppressions they suffered, and did all in his power to help them. Doubtless this sympathy with them was one of the reasons why he was so unpopular with their military and civil masters.

As the delightful cold season of the Bihar uplands passed away and the dry hot winds of upper India began to scorch its plains, the solitary man began to think it 'impossible I could ever subsist long in such a climate.' His inherited tuberculosis became rapidly worse after April 1807, though he reproached himself for lassitude and comparative idleness and put himself under additional pressure to work and pray unceasingly. From this time onwards his journal frequently records sickness, loss of appetite and 'pain' from speaking the Word to people sometimes ending in the temporary loss of his voice altogether. David Brown and Daniel Corrie, among other correspondents, remonstrated with him, the first at a distance and the second from the rock-fortress of Chunar, not far from Dinapore, but Henry met them only occasionally for times of fellowship. 'He needed a watchful and authoritative nurse such as only a wife could be, and he found only lack of sympathy or active opposition. He lived as no man in the tropics in any rank of life should live, from sheer simplicity, unselfishness, and consuming zeal' (*Henry Martyn: Saint and Scholar* p. 210).

In addition, the quiet and lonely evenings gave Henry a chance to sort out his ideas with regard to Cornwall. He alternated between optimism and pessimism about Lydia's arrival, and was often melancholic as he prayed for his dying sister, Laura, and for dear Sally too who he knew was showing signs already of the dreaded family disease.

Top Missionary Priority

As mentioned earlier, Henry's two predecessors as evangelical chaplains were David Brown and Claudius Buchanan. They had arrived in Calcutta in June 1787 and March 1797 respectively and were, like him, graduates of Cambridge. They were also wide-hearted missionary enthusiasts who knew his capacity and were eager to entrust him with the translation of the New Testament into Urdu, Arabic, and Persian. The last of these was spoken at the Mughul Muslim courts in India and was the language of judicial proceedings under the British government in what was then known as Hindustan. It was in June 1807 that they made the definite proposal that he should translate the New Testament into Urdu and supervise translations into Persian and Arabic. They said he should do this with the help of two men they would send him as specialists in these languages: Mirza Mohammed Fitrus of Benares and Nathaniel Sabat, an Arab educated in Baghdad and a former Muslim who had become a Christian three years earlier in Madras at the age of 27[15]. The work became one of his most demanding and time-consuming tasks in Dinapore.

Urdu, the language used by so many millions was not yet standardised, and could boast no single universal work of literature. It was more a spoken language than a literary one, but Henry realised he could bring both aspects together and accepted the request of his elder brethren.

Eventually the black-bearded Nathaniel Sabat arrived and brought with him not only his young and pretty wife Ameena, but also a wild prickly nature that had not yet been wholly refined by grace. He proved both a joy and a trial, a friend and a tormentor to Henry, and many were the storms encountered, as recorded in Henry's journals and some of his friends' records.

Sabat was jealous of Mirza, the Muslim who arrived shortly after him to help with the Urdu translation, and spoke of him with contempt. He was angry that Henry did not hate Mirza too, quoting the Arabic proverb that 'a friend is the enemy of a friend's enemy.' Constant quarrels between Mirza and Sabat hindered progress with the translation work. Henry liked Mirza and found him more accommodating and valuable to the work they were doing together, though the continual conflict between the two helpers caused him distress and drained his physical and mental energy. At last, in spite of his appeals to stay until the translation was finished, Mirza found it impossible to put up the unbalanced Sabat any longer and retreated to Patna. Henry followed him there, and tried to get him to continue with the work, but to no avail. He wrote on 2 May 1808, 'My greatest trial is Sabat, he spreads desolation here. Mirza is driven to Patna, declaring he will not live here to be insulted by Sabat.'

It was Henry's great burden to reach the Muslims. On 30 April 1806, shortly after his arrival in India, he had written words of optimism weighted with realism: 'Even if I never see a native converted, God may design by my patience and continuance in this world to encourage future missionaries. But what surprises me is the change of views I have here from what I had in England. There my heart expanded with hope and joy at the prospect of the speedy conversion of the heathen! But here the sight of the apparent impossibility requires a strong faith to support the spirits.' Many were inspired and stimulated by his example, and so it was after his death that, 'Henry Martyn ... caught the imagination of many missionary-minded people' (Robin E Waterfield, *Christians in Persia* p. 147). Success was not Henry's first criterion but faithfulness to what he knew to be the will of God. (see Matt. 25:23; 1 Cor. 4:2; Heb. 11:5 – activity must never be a substitute for true piety). For the late eminent historian of Christian missionary movements, Kenneth S. Latourette, 'No Protestant missionary to India was better remembered. The combination of rare ability and his devotion which he displayed in a day of

***Benares on the left bank of the River Ganges,
in the early 19th century***

A complete and honest appraisal of the situation when Henry went to India must take into account the bitter hostility towards missionaries displayed by those in power. The British flag became a rallying point where missionaries could find protection in the years after Henry passed away, but earlier on it was often a symbol of hatred and suspicion for any work which brought the gospel to the indigenous people, whether Hindus or Muslims.

pioneering had a profound effect on successive generations of missionaries' (Kenneth S. Latourette, *A History of the Expansion of Christianity* Vol. 6, p.102).

Henry's involvement in public discussions with the

Muslims represents the beginning of a 19th century apologetic approach. In spite of his sensitive personality, he was inevitably drawn into the so-called 'controversy with Islam.' In our present day it might be called public debate, but controversy remains the more accurate description. William Carey, who was delighted with Henry and declared that wherever he was no other missionary would be needed, got wind of the frequent lively public disputes and advised him in December 1808, 'not to argue with the Muslim scholars.' (*Journals and Letters*, Vol. 2, pp. 232f.) Henry's zeal for the Gospel, humble spirit full of grace, and facility with languages equipped him to be a missionary. But nevertheless in his position he was provoked to refutation of Islam and could not avoid a defence of the Christian faith. Moreover, for a Muslim or a Hindu the failure to make an apology was tantamount to a denial of one's faith (see Acts 28:22-24).

One of the main topics of discussion in which Henry was often engaged, both in India and Persia, was the question of miracles, especially the alleged miracles of Mohammed. Henry took his stand in this matter on Mohammed's clear unequivocal disclaimer in the Koran (Surah 29:48-50, 28:48, 49). His patience was often exasperated by the Muslims' rejection of facts and their tendency to use absurd reasoning to maintain their position. In the course of these meetings, he learned more and more about the Muslims and how best to approach them. He said: 'Above all things, seriousness in argument with them seems most desirable, for without it they laugh away the clearest proofs. Zeal for making proselytes they are used to, and generally attribute to a false motive; but a tender concern manifested for their souls is certainly new to them, and seemingly produces corresponding seriousness in their minds' (*Henry Martyn: Saint and Scholar* p. 217). But he also acknowledged that soberness and persuasion alone were not enough (see Acts 24:24, 25; 26:28, 29; 28:22-24).

Earlier at Dinapore, he had questioned the validity of a controversial approach. On 28 April 1807, he noted, 'For myself,

An oriental discussion
We can well imagine Henry discussing matters with Muslims in the oriental fashion illustrated here: cross-legged on a carpet, leaning on cushions. On arrival in Persia he too had a beard, a sign of respectable manhood in some parts of the Islamic world.

I never enter into a dispute with them without having reason to reflect that I mar the work for which I contend by the spirit in which I do it ... They mean to have sent down the leading man from Benares to convince me of the truth of their religion. I wish a spirit of enquiry may be excited, but I lay not much stress upon clear arguments; the work of God is seldom wrought in this way. To preach the Gospel, with the Holy Spirit sent down from heaven, is a better way to win their souls.' This is a good principle for any evangelist, and one which later won unprecedented respect for Henry among the learned Muslims of Persia.[16] Many talks with Muslims helped him to develop a knowledge of Islam and a sensitive approach to them. As pointed out by the late L. Bevan Jones, 'Henry Martyn knew the strain and the struggle to communicate the Gospel to the Muslims, the hope and disappointments that accompany this task in India as well as in Persia' (L Bevan Jones, *People of the Mosque*, p. 315).

Among the many futile attempts of men and women to work out their own salvation, Henry more and more saw the glory of Christ and tried by all means to bring it to those around him. Many of them were willing to argue, some too willing, but they were perplexed and a little annoyed when he inevitably brought the discussion down to the Word of Scripture, and here it was that the arguments usually ended.

With an utter disregard for his own health and strength, Henry applied himself to the work of getting the Word of God into the languages of the natives and becoming more qualified for preaching to them as the Lord led him. The pressure of responsibility was so heavy upon him that he was constantly blaming and judging himself for the lack of capacity and consequent success which he felt in every effort. During his service at Dinapore and its surroundings, he pondered on the size and population of India and his failure to convince any Muslim at the end of his term there. It seemed the most fertile of fields for a missionary and yet overwhelming for one still lacking confidence and assertiveness.

---

[10] The name given to the Netherlands by the French. It was conquered in 1794/95 by General Pichegru (1761-1804) and transformed into a democratic republic in May 1795. Later Napoleon made it the Kingdom of Holland for the benefit of his brother Louis from 1806 to 1810. It was annexed to the French Empire until 1813.

[11] Consider in the light of this statement the eulogy of Jesus about John the Baptist: 'He was the burning and shining light' (Jn. 5:35). John was a wick, and a wick only exists to be burnt up – he was a young man aflame for God who was wholly consumed. Jim Elliot, one of the five young men who laid down their lives in 1956 to reach the Auca Indians of Ecuador with the gospel, was of a similar cast. When a student of 21 in 1948, he wrote in his diary: 'God I pray thee, light these idle sticks of my life and may I burn up for Thee. Consume my life, my God, for it is Thine. I seek not a long life but a full one, like you Lord Jesus.' – 'Am I ignitable? God deliver me from the dread asbestos of "other things." Saturate me with the oil of the Spirit that I may be aflame. But flame is transient, often short-lived. Canst thou bear this my soul? Short life? Make me Thy fuel, Flame of God.' (Elliot, Elisabeth *Shadow of the Almighty* London: Hodder & Stoughton, 1958, pp. 54, 58 & 248.)

[12] William Carey arrived in India in 1793 at the age of 32, to commence 41 years of unbroken service against many odds and adversities; one of the most significant ministries recorded in modern missionary annals. When he landed in Bengal, he was in effect an 'illegal alien' and liable at any moment to deportation. He could not work in British India because of the opposition of the East India Company. They did not want missionaries there upsetting local beliefs and practices because it might have been bad for their business. The obstacles presented by the Company's hostility to evangelical groups both delayed and diverted early plans to open a mission field in northern India. Although a handful of Protestant missionaries had been active in parts of southern India during the eighteenth century, the East India Company made strenuous efforts to prevent the settlement of any such missionaries in its Bengal Presidency. The newcomers, a trio under the auspices of the newly-founded English Baptist Missionary Society (1792), realised their safety would lie in settling at Serampore, the tiny Danish colony about 15 miles from Calcutta. It was only as the years passed that a more favourable atmosphere for missionary work developed. When William Carey died on 9 June 1834 at almost 73, he had superintended the translation of the whole Bible into five languages, Bengali among them, and parts of the Bible into 29 other languages. He had also undertaken many other activities. For these reasons he is considered the 'father of modern missions' by a number of Christian historians. However, it could be argued that he followed the missionary drive pioneered by the pietistic Moravian movement under the godly leadership of the German, Count Ludwig von Zinzendorf (1700-1760).

[13] Francis Xavier was a Spanish Jesuit. He was sent from the city of Goa under the patronage of John III, the King of Portugal, to Janhangir (1569-1627), the great Mughul ruler of India. He presented an apologia or treatise which had taken him 12 years to write in Lahore: 'A Mirror for Showing Truth'. This is more to do with the practice of the Roman Catholic church than Christianity itself.

[14] John B. Gilchrist was a surgeon with the East India Company and an early teacher of Hindustani in Calcutta between 1783-1804. His dictionary and grammar were printed there during his stay.

[15] The story of Nathaniel Sabat is told in chapter two of my book in Norwegian called *Fra Islam til Golgata*, published by Luther Forlag in 1982 and in *Crusaders of the Twentieth Century* by Rev. W. A. Rice, London: Church Missionary Society, 1910, pp. 73, 74. The account of how he became a Christian is quite dramatic, and there is some controversy about the way his life ended. Whether he ever returned to the Christianity he recanted from or not is a matter of debate, but we can be sure the Lord knows.

[16] The land known in the West as Persia has always been Iran for its peoples. At the wish of the Shah, Réza Pahlévi, who reigned from 1925 to1941, Iran was substituted for Persia in 1935 as the name to be used for the country throughout the world. No attempt has been made to change the name in this book since the land was Persia to Henry Martyn.

4
TRIUMPHING OVER ADVERSITIES

Fateful Transfer to Cawnpore

In April 1809, after two and half years at Dinapore, Henry was transferred by the military authorities to Cawnpore in the Mughul heartland (modern-day Kanpur in Uttar Pradesh state)[17]. It was the worst time of the year to travel, but Henry was impatient to start his new assignment and foolishly travelled as quickly as possible. He had been badly advised about the way to travel and went by palanquin or covered litter carried by relays of Indian porters, rather than the slower river route up the Ganges. It was a journey of over 300 miles, and although at first he travelled in the cool of the night there was no way of escaping the torrid heat between Allahbad and Cawnpore. He covered the last stretch of about 120 miles travelling for two days and nights without any proper break. The jolting palanquin was wide open to the scorching hot winds, which raised dust and dried out his throat and his skin. This terrible journey must have done some long term damage to his fit but now rather fragile body. The occasional torrential rains cooled the burning inferno for a while but provided no relief for a man subject to tuberculosis. The trying climate of heat and humidity undermined his health; the dusty air especially proved very harmful to his lungs. The disease which caused the death of his half-sister Laura during 1807 began to ravage his frail body, and the entries in his journals which referred to pain grew more frequent. Cawnpore was the worst post in the country for a man in his state of health, so this was an ominous beginning.

Henry took four services each Sunday, and spent long but most enjoyable hours working on his texts. He was often in great pain and close to fainting as his lungs plagued him more and more, especially when debilitating heat-waves and dusty winds turned Cawnpore into a cauldron. Taking refuge in his house at midday did not help because the hot sun filtered through the double doors and window shutters of green latticework, sapping his energy. But the call of the Lord Jesus forced him to speak as loudly and persuasively as possible to Europeans and natives even if he could barely manage to whisper after a sermon, as he confessed to David Brown and Daniel Corrie. Despite his zeal, his days of public preaching were virtually at an end, and with it the melodious singing sound of his voice, which slowly weakened till it seemed as if it would vanish.

Henry saw as little lasting result from his open-air preaching to the natives in the suffocating whirl of dust storms here as he had from much of his pastoral work elsewhere in India. He lamented that the whole enterprise of coming to the subcontinent was useless, but he was wrong in this. Preaching in the bazaars, which he was in two minds about anyway, was not tolerated by the East India Company. As a result he confined himself to regular addresses to the Indians who gathered voluntarily in his own private compound. As he preached to them one

*Cawnpore – 'the threshold of misery',
in the early 19th century*

day in the courtyard of his house, a group of Muslims stood in a row in front of him showing their disdain for a message they regarded as heretical nonsense. But one of the group, Sheikh Saleh (1776-1827), had his curiosity aroused by the thin 'beardless boy'. He was a zealous and influential Muslim teacher in Lucknow and a native of Delhi, but was disillusioned with Islam. Hearing Henry preach on the Ten Commandments, he was attracted by the idea that the law needed to be interpreted in the light of the Sermon on the Mount. He was also struck by a message and appeal which could be presented with such conviction to a hostile audience. He therefore made contact with the preacher, who recruited him on to his translating staff. They started to have private conversations in the peaceful atmosphere of Henry's bungalow.

When this sincere seeker was entrusted with the newly-finished Urdu New Testament (not the Persian one as related in George Smith's biography, p. 286), he started to read it from Matthew to Revelation. The Word of God fell on prepared ground, and he became a Christian proving again that, 'Faith comes by hearing, and hearing by the word of God' (Rom. 10:17, see also Jn. 6:44, 45). Saleh was baptised in Calcutta in 1811 by David Brown as Abdul Masih (meaning 'Servant of Christ') and proved a great force for his Master in India. He became a notable Christian leader who lived for 15 years after Henry's death, labouring among his Muslim compatriots (a striking watercolour of Abdul Masih found its way to England from India and now hangs in the director's office of the Henry Martyn Centre in Cambridge). Daniel Corrie wrote the following to Charles Simeon in 1823 referring to Henry: 'Could he look from heaven and see Abdul Masih with the translated New Testament in his hand, preaching to the listening throng … It would add fresh delight to his holy soul' (George E and H Corrie, *Memoirs of the Right Rev Daniel Corrie* p. 250). Corrie and Abdul Masih became great friends and enjoyed each other's company in deep spiritual fellowship; perhaps Henry's 'convert' became the friend Corrie lost in Henry. He accompanied Corrie up the Ganges to his posting at Agra in 1813 and both of them witnessed spiritual breakthroughs, at least initially. Corrie left the following year, but Abdul Masih stayed until 1825.

Near the end of 1809, news reached Henry of his sister Sally's death despite his many prayers for her recovery. He wrote to her young husband, recognising his loss as even greater than his own. But he had now lost both his parents and both his sisters without being at their bedsides, and it was coming home to him that he would soon die from the same dreadful disease as well. His half-brother John, who was 15 years older than Henry and married, was also struck by the fatal scourge in 1811. The all-too-fleeting transience of human life was a very common theme in his thoughts especially during his illnesses in India and his dreadful fevers in Persia. When later he saw the ancient Persian city of Persepolis, the sight reinforced these feelings about the brevity of life and his own in particular. This may explain the very strong urge he had to see his translations of the New Testament published and circulated as soon as possible, whatever the cost might be in terms of his health and survival.

Henry's health became so bad that he had to reduce his speaking engagements after just a year of service in Cawnpore. He also found little strength for his other duties, and had to confess to his friends, David Brown and Daniel Corrie, that his chest pains were starting to alarm him. On 16 April 1810, we read in a letter to David Brown in which he mentions the deterioration of his health, 'Pray for me. Prayer lengthened Hezekiah's life, perhaps it may mine.' It was around that time that Daniel, who had been appointed chaplain to Chunar, was transferred to Agra and passed through Cawnpore on his way to his new posting. While stopping there he realised Henry's critical condition and asked the General to let him to stay much longer than had been contemplated, which was granted. He brought his sister Mary with him, who had come out to India recently to join him, and together they settled down to

Abdul Masih (1776-1827) – 'trophy of God's grace'
This portrait, by an unknown hand, hangs in the Henry Martyn Centre, Cambridge, on loan from Ridley Hall.

look after the invalid. Both proved to be of great support and comfort to Henry, and during that time Mary was clearly very close to him. She was, no doubt, attracted to him, and their marriage may have been a possibility though Henry denied the rumour in his letter to Lydia dated 14 August 1810, which contains the following sentences: 'My heart has not strayed from Marazion … Five long years have passed, and I am still faithful.' John R. Martyn writes in his biography, 'Henry seemed resigned to their earthly separation, and happy with a metaphysical union, and yet his abiding desire was to get back to Cornwall' (*Henry Martyn (1781-1812), scholar and missionary to India and Persia: a biography* p. 112).

Already before his departure from England, Henry's diary contains hints of the probability of an early death. Daniel Corrie, well aware of his precarious condition while visiting and assisting him in Dinapore after the first and almost fatal attack, recorded in September 1808, 'He wished, if it pleases God, to be spared on account of the translation' (*Memoirs of the Right Rev Daniel Corrie,* p. 118). And now Henry realised: 'My strength for public preaching is gone, but to translate the Word of God is a work of more lasting benefit than my preaching would be.' To David Brown he wrote: 'Without the work of translation, I should fear my presence in India were useless.'

His infirmities were not to be a hindrance in pressing on with his calling as a missionary, and he took on this other function to fulfil it through the sufficiency of God's grace. Like Paul with his infirmity (was it a problem with his eyesight or something else? There has been much speculation about the thorn in the flesh. See 2 Cor. 12:7-10), Henry seems to have gone through a similar process of frustration (v. 8), revelation (v. 9) and transformation (v. 10) in triumphing over adversities. Having to bear so many disappointments and trials, he directed his thoughts more than ever to his translations of the New Testament, trying to transcend his intense grief.

Mrs. Mary Sherwood's Impressions

Henry was forced to leave Cawnpore in October 1810 for medical reasons, but throughout his 18 month stay there was happy in having a Christian home constantly open to him. Mr. and Mrs.

Henry Sherwood of the King's 53rd Regiment were friends with whom he had been closely acquainted already when they were stationed in Dinapore. They had supported him there, and it was they who nursed him back to a measure of health in Cawnpore. Mary Martha Sherwood (1775-1851) gained fame as an author of children's books. Her autobiography was compiled by her daughter, Sophia Kelly, from the diaries she and her husband left. These provide a fascinating picture of Henry and of those around him, and of the atmosphere of India during this critical time of his life there. Here is her impression of him: 'His features were not regular, but the expression was so luminous, so intellectual, so affectionate, so beaming with divine charity, that no one could have looked at his features and thought of their shape and forms; the out-beaming of his soul would absorb the attention of every observer ... The conversion of the native, and the building up of the kingdom of Christ, were the great objects for which alone that child of God seemed to exist ... Henry Martyn was one of the very few persons whom I ever met who appeared never to be drawn

Mary Sherwood (1775-1851)

away from one leading and prevailing object of interest, and that object was the expansion of Christianity. He is one of the most pleasing, mild, and heavenly-minded men, walking in this turbulent world with peace in his mind and charity in his heart' (S. Kelly, *The Life of Mrs Sherwood ... with Extracts from Mr Sherwood's Journal during his Imprisonment in France and residence in India* pp. 317-321).

Henry's journals are marked by the rather sombre tone of what was meant to be the secret record of the state of his soul with God. They need to be balanced by an account of his manner of life among his friends from the hands of one who knew him intimately. It is for this reason that *The Life and Times of Mrs. Captain Henry Sherwood* (edited by J. Harvey Darton using material from the Sherwoods' diaries and published in 1910) is so valuable. For while Sir John William Kaye (1814-1876) has given us one of the best analyses of Henry's character in his *Christianity in India* published in 1859, this is not a personal first-hand impression for the author was born two years after Henry passed away. Mrs. Sherwood gives a much more vivid and lucid account of the man than his own personal notes convey, though she did not share all his views. She and a few other close acquaintances provide a quite different impression of Henry's character and bearing than the one we get from his own journal and letters. No doubt they counterbalance each other to produce a truer description of his personality with its light and shadow than we would get if we had only one or the other. Mary Sherwood's literary ability and keen observation are particularly helpful in coming to a right evaluation and appreciation of the young missionary. 'Only towards himself was he merciless, and sometimes his self-condemnation seems to be outside the bounds of common sense,' remarked one of his later biographers, Kellsye M. Finnie (Kellsye M. Finnie, *Beyond the Minarets; a biography of Henry Martyn* p.67). Captain Sherwood, his wife and children gave Henry more of the joy of home life than he had known elsewhere in India except with David Brown and his family. Mary noted: 'Henry could be very serious, but when he relaxed, he used to play and laugh like an innocent, happy child, especially if children were present to play and laugh with him.' And so impressed was this family by his character and their memory of him that they named their second son Henry, born in the spring of 1813.

Practical righteousness and personal holiness in his actions and thoughts meant nothing less than the long steadfast effort to remove and disown both sins and self so that Christ might reign as Lord of all (see Jn. 3:30). On 24 September 1807, he expressed this ideal from a new point of view: 'To live without sin is what I can not expect in this world, but to desire to live without it may be the experience of every hour' (*Journals and Letters*, Vol. 2, p. 109). Indeed there is a difference between the sad acknowledgement that we sin daily and the idea that, because we do so, such sinning is acceptable! Henry had a rare degree of that crystalline purity of heart that is proof of the consecration to God of mind and manhood.

In Cawnpore, Henry had two houses near one another, both with verandas: one for himself after his short convalescence in the Sherwoods' home and a smaller one for Nathaniel Sabat and his wife who had come to join him. At first Sabat settled down with a mind to work, helping with the translations into Arabic and Persian, but when the novelty of his new house wore off, he lapsed into apathy. He became capricious and eager to find any excuse to shut up his books, being satisfied to get through just one chapter a day. Henry was also starting to question the quality of his co-worker's Persian, but any criticism only made him hysterical. Then Henry heard from Mirza that he was willing to come back to help in the work provided Sabat was not around. Although this meant constant vigilance on the part of the harassed peace-maker, he felt it worthwhile to secure the help of this valuable language teacher once again. This enabled the translation of the Urdu New Testament to be taken forward in earnest. Henry was perhaps too busy with the work to realise how sick he really was, and left almost all of the worrying to his friends. But attacks of pain, loss of his voice and frequent spells of total exhaustion warned him of the onset of his tuberculosis.

Excitement and Reservation

Philology so gripped Henry that often he could not sleep thinking of some connections between Hebrew and Persian word-forms: 'I made some discovery respecting the Hebrew verb, but was unfortunately so much delighted that I could not sleep, in consequence of which I have had a headache ever since.' 'One night I didn't sleep a wink. Knowing what would be the consequence the next day, I struggled hard, and turned every way, that my mind might be delivered from what was before it, but all in vain. One discovery succeeded another, in Hebrew, Arabic, and Greek, so rapidly that I was sometimes in an ecstasy.' More delightful even than philology in the abstract was the work of translation when the subject was nothing less than the Word of God. 'What do I owe to the Lord, for permitting me to take part in a translation of His Word? Never did I see so much wonder and wisdom and love in the Blessed Book, as since I have been obliged to study every expression; and it is a delightful reflection that death can not deprive us of the pleasure of studying its mysteries.' No wonder a man with such a perception of the value of the Bible was willing to produce the best possible translation, and never tired of the book!

As George Smith pertinently wrote, 'The brief decade of Henry Martyn's working life fell at a time when the science of Comparative Philology was as yet unborn, but the materials were almost ready for generalisation' (*Henry Martyn: Saint and Scholar* p. 425).

His first draft of the New Testament in Urdu was subjected to rigorous revision before his own critical judgment was satisfied. But finally, to his great delight, at the close of the year 1810, it was received and acclaimed by the most competent authorities of the day in Calcutta. After only three years of intensive work, triumphing over all the adversities, the Urdu

Prayer

Henry's life and ministry were characterised by prayer showing his total dependence on the Lord.[18]

New Testament was completed and ready for the press. But Mirza Fitrus, Henry's valuable collaborator, was a Muslim, and though he had had long conversations with him about Islam and Christianity he presented throughout a pathetic picture of doubt and uncertainty. Henry's efforts to win him to Christ were endless, but when they finally parted Mirza was still in an agnostic state. It seemed that he was one of those to whom 'the gospel was preached ... but the word which they heard did not profit them, not being mixed with faith' (Heb. 4:2).

There was great satisfaction among the experts in Calcutta with the Urdu New Testament. There was also hope for the Arabic, but the Persian was found to have too many Arabic idioms in it to be a realistic proposition for average readers. Henry also realised that Sabat's grammar in the Arabic translation needed more attention. It was impossible, however, to convince the bombastic Arab of anything found wanting and requiring improvement. Henry was very much a perfectionist, very hard working and determined never to publish anything prematurely, despite the urgency to have the work done. During his posting in Dinapore, he had been reluctant to make gifts of the gospels in Urdu to his Muslim contacts until he was sure that the translation had been carefully checked.

Matthew 11:28-30 in Arabic calligraphy

some years in Persia, he had appeared to the Calcutta chaplains to be the ideal man for the job. Needless to say, he shared their opinion. One of his odd and presumptuous ideas was that he was under the immediate influence and direction of the Holy Spirit to such an extent there would not be one single error in the whole of the Persian translation, which was largely his work. He was 'prodigiously proud' of it, and Henry at first accepted his opinion. But when the two translations reached Calcutta, a competent committee was not at all complimentary and started to question and criticise the work. Sabat's Arabic grammar was loose, and his Persian too stilted and full of Arabic words to appeal to a native Persian. He, of course, was furious about their comments, but Henry would never accept second-best. He gradually became convinced that truly idiomatic translations could not be made except in Arabia and

Persia, just as his own Urdu translation had been done so well in India. His gentleness and forbearance never shone more brightly than in his treatment of Sabat, but his disappointment lent urgency necessity to the idea of a visit to the countries where the language in question was spoken. He decided to go to Arabia with Sabat to complete his Arabic translation. Until the end Henry's patience was tested by this extraordinary man. He remained volatile and unpredictable, an extremely unbalanced person with a loud voice and an explosive temperament. This proved, again and again, a great trial to the sensitive and somewhat reserved young European. Though Henry still sought Sabat's participation, the debate over the quality and acceptability of his work so far made him terribly upset and he started to speak against Christianity. With his heart burning with rage and his great voice thundering with anger, Sabat left his friends, bringing to an end his collaboration with Henry. He stubbornly went aboard a ship and sailed down the Bay of Bengal by the Indo-Chinese coast until he came to Penang in Malaysia where he began to live as a trader. According to some sources which are still controversial, he backslid in heart for several years but then repented, finding spiritual restoration under God's sovereign discipline (see Jer. 2:19, 3:22; Ps. 119:71, 75; Heb. 12:7-11). According to Colonel MacInnes of Penang, as recorded in the *Memoir of the Rev. Thomas Thomason*: 'Sabat never spoke of Mr. Martyn without the most profound respect, and shed tears of grief whenever he recalled how severely he had tried the patience of this faithful servant of God.'

Leaving Cawnpore down the Ganges river, Henry was upset to see how few of the soldiers at Berhampore had stayed faithful to Christ, as only nine joined him for hymn singing on board. He was also disturbed to find in all the places where he had been posted, British men living with native women in immoral relationships. As the boat left the Ganges it was towed down the Hooghly, reaching Calcutta on 10 November 1810. Henry felt almost the same sensation as a homeward-bound British traveller might have on getting his first glimpse of the white cliffs of Dover. It was a long four years since he had been in Calcutta and Aldeen, and he was exhilarated to meet old friends again and their children, especially the Brown children with whom he had had such fun; he had never stopped cherishing his times with them. Among these friends was Thomas Thomason who, like Daniel Corrie, had been inspired by Henry's example. An intimate friend of Henry's, he gave up in middle age a comfortable home in the pleasant vicinity of Cambridge and accepted a post as chaplain in Bengal, taking his family with him when he was posted to Calcutta in 1808. Later he undertook the supervision of the translation of the Old Testament into Urdu.

The Thomasons were taken aback by the great change in Henry's looks, now so thin and sallow as he sat on their sofa, but telling them about his ambitious plans with sparkling eyes. A few days later, knowing how concerned Henry's acquaintances in England were about his physical condition,

Thomas Thomason (1774-1829)

Thomason wrote an interesting letter to Charles Simeon, whose curate he once had been, to describe their impression of his old friend: 'Martyn is on his way to Arabia, where he is going in pursuit of health and knowledge ... He has some great plan in mind, of which I am not a competent judge, but as far as I do understand it, the object is far too grand for one short life, and much beyond his feeble and exhausted frame. Feeble it is indeed! How fallen and changed! His complaint lies in his lungs.' In spite of his own worries, Thomason ended his briefing on a more positive note: 'But let us hope that the sea-air may revive him, and continue his life for many years. In all respects, he is exactly the same as he was: he shines in all the dignity of love, and seems to carry about him such a heavenly majesty as impresses the mind beyond description. But if he talks much, though in low voice, he sinks, and you are reminded of his being "dust and ashes."' Thomason seems to have agreed with Henry's talk of a milder and healthier climate in Persia, which he saw in poetic colours, according to Mary Sherwood, as a land of roses, flowing streams and perfumed breezes. Perhaps he thought of it as a paradise garden and hoped it might prove an elixir of recovery. As researcher Barbara Eaton wrote: 'Henry may have played down his poor health in letters to Lydia but it was a cause for concern to friends in Calcutta, who now saw for themselves how ill he had become. Their concern was still further increased by his apparent disregard for it with his plan to travel to Persia' (Barbara Eaton, *Letters to Lydia – 'Beloved Persis'* p. 166).

During the time of waiting at Calcutta for a ship to bring him round the Indian subcontinent to a healthier climate, Henry was able to fulfil a five-year old promise to Charles Simeon to have his portrait painted and sent to England.[19] When David Brown saw it, he commented that it was a striking likeness of his friend, but added, 'That is not the Martyn who arrived in India; it is Martyn the recluse' (Constance Padwick, *Henry Martyn: confessor of the faith* p. 131). When later Simeon saw it he was distressed to see the change in his former curate:

'I could not bear to look upon it, but turned away and went to a distance, covering my face, and in spite of every effort to the contrary, crying aloud with anguish ... In seeing how much he is worn I am constrained to call to my relief the thought of Whose service he has worn himself so much' (*Charles Simeon* p. 108). Indeed the sickness and hard toil had left their imprint on Henry's youthful face.

In his last sermon at Calcutta, Henry called for consistent obedience to the biblical commission of Christ and urged all Christians in India to launch a programme of Scripture distribution in conjunction with the British and Foreign Bible Society (his text was 'one thing needful,' and a copy of the discourse is in the British Library in London). Although Warren Hastings, Governor General of India from 1773 until 1785, had once dismissed a chaplain for distributing evangelistic tracts and proselytising, Henry dared to advocate from the pulpit and in private conversations the proclamation of the gospel to the natives. According to his vision and against all odds, he called for missions, urging full Christian participation. Yet generally speaking he found little support among his parishioners: 'They considered his preaching to Indians politically dangerous and socially insulting to "the ruling race!"' (Archibald McLean, *Epoch makers of modern missions*). Nevertheless, he pursued his work among the local population at his various postings though he constantly had to defend doing so before his fellow countrymen, especially officials (it must be said that colonial rule, whether British, French or Dutch, was not always synonymous with Christian missions). However, as we have seen, there were other evangelical chaplains of the same mind – David Brown, Claudius Buchanan, Daniel Corrie, Thomas Thomason – if only a handful. They were not satisfied to confine themselves to ministering to the needs of their European congregations in the various stations where they were posted, but had begun to disseminate copies of the gospels and take cautious steps towards making contacts among non-Christians. If these activities were somewhat clandestine, and disapproved of by the

East India Company, they were undertaken in anticipation of a lifting of the embargo on missionary activities. It is significant that just as the campaign to allow missionary work among the Indian population was gathering momentum in England with the renewal of the East India Company's Charter in Parliament in 1813, Henry, as chaplain of the company, had already quietly, and sometimes openly, engaged in reaching the natives with the gospel. The change effected in the company, one year after his passing away, was followed by a striking increase of Protestant missions in India.

New Horizons: Arabia and Persia

On 11 January 1811, the lonely Henry slipped away from Calcutta to avoid another painful and distressing farewell. He embarked on the ship *Ahmoody*, and reached Bombay (the trading port between Great Britain and the rest of India) about 46 days later. His time at sea was consumed by linguistic studies and the reading of *Travels through Arabia* (1792) by Carsten Niebuhr. As the ship docked in Bombay on his birthday, he wrote gloomily: 'This day I finish the thirtieth year of my unprofitable life, an age in which Brainerd had finished his course. He gained about a hundred savages to the Gospel. I can scarcely number the twentieth part.' Such feelings are typical of someone who is introverted, and demonstrate his humanity (what a snare, and how degrading it can be, to compare ourselves to or compete with one another! See 2 Cor. 10:12). After a while, Henry obtained a passage on a ship of the East India Company, the *Benares*, escorted by a warship, the *Prince of Wales*, which was stationed in the Persian Gulf to root out any Arab pirates operating along the coast of Oman. The *Benares* was on its way to Persia and Henry was to act as chaplain to all the Europeans on board. So after a little less than five years spent in India, he left the country where he had fully intended to spend his whole life – partly because his health was broken and partly because he wanted to correct any imperfections in his translations of the New Testament.

We read in a letter from Cawnpore, dated October 1809: 'Thus we are baffled – yet it is the Lord's will and therefore I feel willing to try again and again, till the Word is approved … The Arabic translation of the Scripture is the most important version of all, Arabic being understood by the major part of the Muslim world.' Again: 'If my life is spared there is no reason why the New Testament in Arabic should not be done in Arabia and the Persian in Persia – Arabia shall hide me till I come forth with an approved New Testament in Arabic.' His request to be dismissed from clerical duties and granted sick-leave had been accepted by the colonial authorities, and this allowed him to concentrate on translation work. 'Study never makes me ill, scarcely ever fatigues me. But my lungs! Death is seated there; it is speaking that kills me.' So he wrote to Lydia in April 1810 (*Journals and Letters*, Vol. 2, p. 294).

Arabia was the cradle of Islam, and no missionary had yet carried out even a token visit there as a testimony to the gospel. But in January 1811 Henry was confident enough to write, 'I now pass from India to Arabia, not knowing what things shall befall me there' *(Journals and Letters*, Vol. 2, p. 326). He did not know that the history of direct effort to reach the great Arabian peninsula with the gospel was to begin with him. At the end of April 1811, he landed at the port of the Sultanate of Muscat. This was surrounded by a semi-circle of mountains but otherwise was situated in a monotonous landscape, which he described in a letter to Lydia: 'to judge from the aspect of the country it has little pretensions to the name [Felix or Happy Arabia]; unless burning barren rocks convey the idea of felicity; but perhaps as there is a promise in reserve for the sons of Joktan their land may one day be blessed indeed' (Joktan was the son of Eber and of the family of Shem (Gen. 10:25, 26, 29; 1 Chron. 1:19, 20, 23). His descendants can be traced to southern Arabia as explained in my Norwegian book: *Elsk disse araberne – Gud's løfer blir virkeliggjort* (Love Those Arabs

– God's Promises Unfold). He took some strolls through the noisy and smelly bazaar, both impressed and squeezed by the crowds. Muscat in Oman was to be the only part of Arabian soil on which he would stand and stay. Nevertheless, he was to be the scout marking the trail for modern missionary work in Arabia in more ways than one. Muscat was the first step on his journey to Persia, and then Damascus and Baghdad; he spent only five days there but the prayers he offered during that time were to find an answer in God's providence subsequently, and his visit was a breakthrough after many years of neglect of the need of the Muslim population. One evening, an Arab soldier and his slave came on board the ship to bid him farewell. Henry wrote, 'They asked me to see the Gospel. The instant I gave them a copy in Arabic, the poor boy began to read, and

A view of Muscat harbour by R Temple, 1810
The entrance into the harbour from the ocean offers an impressive spectacle of high barren rocks and the landmark of a 16th century Portuguese fort.

carried it off as a great prize, which I hope he will find it to be.'

Samuel M. Zwemer (1867-1952), pioneer-missionary in Arabia, said: 'The facts about Martyn's life show at how many points it touched Arabia; his purpose, his prayers, his studies, his translation, and his visit to Muscat, but more than all there was the result for Arabia of Martyn's influence and power to inspire others' (Samuel M. Zwemer, *Arabia; the Cradle of Islam*, p. 319).

From the eastern coast of Arabia, Henry sailed across the Gulf of Oman with its notorious winds. On 21 May, four weeks after leaving Muscat, he landed in Persia at the shimmering harbour of Bushire. It was almost the hottest time of the year, as it had been when he made the trip to Cawnpore which so damaged his health, but he had to press on. He was blazing a path as the first Protestant missionary in Persia. He stayed in Bushire for ten days, living with an English merchant and his Armenian wife as he prepared for his journey. He was drawn to the Armenian community in the town, partly due to their victimisation by the followers of Islam. He also felt sorry for the Jews in the country who shared the same fate. During his time there, he ordered a typical Persian outfit, but perhaps a still greater change was to let his beard and moustache grow for his travel inland. On 30 May 1811, he set out in a caravan. An Armenian servant, taken from the warship, escorted him on a mule, and another carried his books. Though refreshed by the long sea voyage, the nine-day journey overland to Shiraz was very tiring for him. It followed one of the roughest caravan tracks and some of the most precipitous mountain passes in Persia and this sapped his strength even more. They travelled by night because the daytime was intolerably hot. The caravan of 30 horses and mules filed out on to a barren, sandy plain, which stretched 100 miles to the Persian plateau. The starlight, tinkling bells on mules, and muleteer's plaintive love-song, gave the caravan a magical appeal. But at daybreak they were still on the plain, and it was like being in a blaze. Henry had to find the shadow

Shiraz – 'the city of predilection'

of some trees to pitch his small tent and rest as best as he could. On 2 June, they began the long climb up four long steep passes. At night, on the mountain plateau, 1,400 feet above sea level it was bitterly cold. On 7 June, they left the Zagros mountains and entered the green valley of Dustarjan. After two more nights of riding, with the exhausted rider permanently in danger of falling from his horse, they reached the gate of Shiraz. Within a week he began his Persian translation of the New Testament, and completed 'the happy toil' in February the following year.

Though Persia was overwhelmingly Muslim, chiefly of the Shiite branch of Islam, Christian minorities such as the Nestorian and Armenian communities were to be found. Henry was the first Protestant evangelical missionary to reside in the country. Coming to another culture, he adopted the Persian dress of baggy blue trousers, red boots, tunic and coat, and an enormous woolly sheepskin cone on the head. He was a stranger in a strange land with only memories of all he had left to keep him company. He thought affectionately of

God's mercy and love (see Rom. 8:1 'no condemnation' and 8:38, 39 'no separation').

Henry's health had improved a little since his arrival in Shiraz. Regular exercise, good nutritious food, the comfort of soft cushions and carpets in the tent set up in the garden where he found coolness, peace and tranquillity amid clusters of grapes beside a clear stream, all contributed to this. It was an ideal sanctuary and a real relief from the extreme heat and dust of Cawnpore. Without sermons to deliver, his voice recovered, though he was still prone to hot flushes and at other times was as pale as death.

Confessor and Contender for the Christian faith

During his months in Shiraz, Henry was constantly beset by Muslim visitors eager to discuss theology with him. There was an extraordinary stir about religion, and he welcomed these enquirers singly or in small groups. He shared with each some truth of the gospel in spite of the pressing translation work and deteriorating health. Sometimes a whole day's work would be suspended as he talked and reasoned with his learned or questioning visitors. The general reaction was one of curiosity and then of frantic defence of Islam and the Koran. But his Christian refutation of Mohammed's claims began to be rumoured around the city, and so tense was the atmosphere that developed as a result of the presence and influence of the zealous Christian that the authorities became concerned. After some deliberation, the Muslims arranged for a treatise, a defence of Islam, to be prepared by Mirza Ibrahim, who was known as the foremost of all the Muslim teachers. When this challenge was presented to Henry with the purpose of silencing him, he replied at once with a masterly series of tracts covering the whole controversy.

All Henry's experience among the Sunni Muslims of Patna and the Shia Muslims of Lucknow in northern India had fitted him for the discussions which were almost forced upon him in

Temporary residence
This was the guest-house in the garden of his host, Jaffir Ali Khan, where Henry lodged during his stay in Shiraz and revised his translation of the Persian New Testament. Today it is known as the Fars Museum where the achievements of famous Persian poets are on display with most likely no reference to Henry Martyn.

Persia. Knowing what to expect before arriving there, he had been reading and studying the Koran afresh on board ship, to help prepare himself for the controversy.

John Malcolm wrote to Gore Ouseley in his letter of introduction for Henry, 'I have not hesitated to tell him that I thought you would require that he should act with great caution, and not allow his zeal to run away with him' (John W Kaye, *Lives of Indian Officers Vol. 2*, p.65). But another has written: 'His zeal did, however, run away with him and he was soon engaged in fierce theological argument with the ulema or religious leaders of Shiraz. During his year there he wrote and distributed tracts in explanation and defence of Christianity, to which the ulema replied with tracts of their own. Yet despite these disputations Martyn, unlike some of the missionaries who were to follow after, seems by his humility and patience to have won the affection of those with whom he argued. They recognised his obvious sincerity and called him "a man of God." Sometimes they came to visit him in such numbers that he had to decline to see them so that he could continue his translation work' (Sir Denis Wright, *The English amongst the Persians during the Qajar period, 1787-1921* p.113).

At one point, so exasperated with rational controversy in Persia, Henry wrote: 'I have now lost all hope of ever convincing Muslims by arguments ... I know not what to do but to pray for them.' His words reflected his dilemma about employing means consistent with his message and goal. The entry in his diary on 8 September 1811 says: 'I do use the means in a certain way, but frigid reasoning with men of perverse minds seldom brings men to Christ. However, as they require it, I reason and accordingly challenged them to prove the divine mission of their prophet. In consequence of this, a learned Arabic treatise was written by one who was considered as the most able man, and put into my hands ... The writer of it said that if I could give satisfactory answer to it he would become a Christian, and at all events would make my reply as public as I pleased. I did answer it and after some faint efforts on his part to defend himself, he acknowledged the force of my arguments, but was afraid to let them be generally known. He then began to inquire about the Gospel, but was not satisfied with my statement. He required me to prove from the very beginning the divine mission of Moses, as well as of Christ; the truth of the Scriptures, etc. With very little hope that any good will come of it, I am now employed in drawing out the evidences of the truth; but oh, that I could converse and reason, and plead with power from on high. How powerless are the best-directed arguments till the Holy Ghost renders them effectual.' But Henry could not extricate himself from his human circumstances, and so he sought to shape an acceptable Christian apologetic.

The whole prolonged debate taught him, with a vivid sense of reality, that the only key to Muslim thought lies in the integrity and authority of Scripture. The mighty weapon which he longed to forge to this end was the New Testament in their own language (see 2 Tim. 3:16; Heb. 4:12, 13). Though very eager to witness and always 'ready to give an answer to every man that asked the reason of his hope' (1 Pet. 3:15), it was the Persian New Testament that was Henry's chief concern. He knew he was a dying man, and that it must be completed while he was still alive. This goal was his raison d'être and a driving force despite his declining energy.

And yet for all his clear vision and heavy burden, Henry's activities were still pervaded by his love for Lydia Grenfell which burned with a steady flame and was never far from his thoughts. It seemed to have come to an end when he received her letter in India on Christmas Day in 1809, but the death of his sister, Sally, led to a fresh correspondence. When writing to console him, Lydia suggested that she might take the place of the beloved sister he had lost and this began a new series of letters between them.

'Since you kindly bid me, my beloved friend, consider you in the place of that dear sister whom it has pleased God in His wisdom to take from me, I gratefully accept the offer of a correspondence, which it has ever been the anxious wish of my heart to establish. Your kindness is the more acceptable because it is shown in the day of affliction. Though I had heard of my dear sister's illness some months before I received the account of her death, and though the nature of her disorder was such as left me not a ray of hope, so that I was mercifully prepared for the event, still the certainty of it fills me with anguish. It is not that she has left me, for I never expected to see her more on earth ... How frightful is the desolation which death makes, and how appalling his visits when it enters one's family ... When month after month passed away, and no letter came from you, I almost abandoned the hope of ever hearing from you again' (March 30th, 1810). He had perhaps ceased to cherish any real hope that he would gain her hand, but her image was still in the background of all his dreams. He felt like a man who could not have her with him, and yet did not know how to live without her. Departing from India, he started to write letters to her again in the midst of fears, frustrated hopes, regrets and unfulfilled longings (see Prov. 13:12a). In Shiraz, he was still embracing his beloved Lydia in his thoughts; still longing to have her beside him as his wife.

He wrote to her on 8 September and 21 October 1811 with a heart sore with loneliness and love, telling her that he was thinking of her incessantly and requesting her prayers.

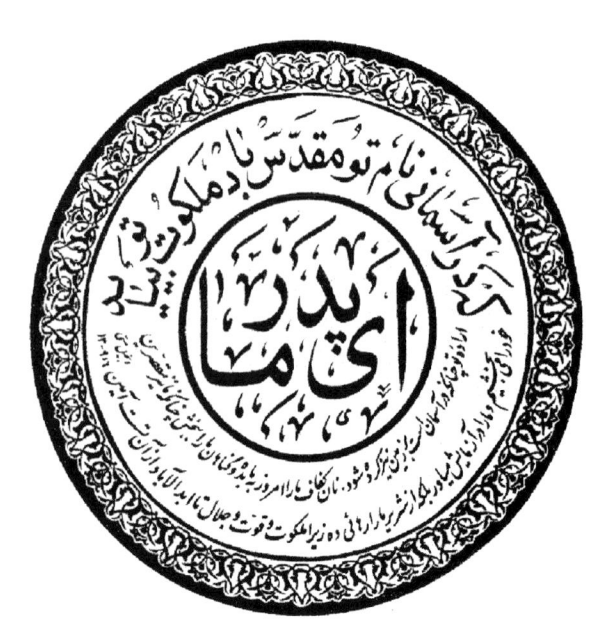

The disciples' prayer, often called the Lord's Prayer, (Matthew 6:9-13) in Persian calligraphy

Jubilant Release: The Persian New Testament

18 February 1812 was to be his last birthday. He wrote in his journal: 'This is my birthday, on which I complete my thirty-first year. The Persian New Testament has begun, and I may say finished as only the last eight chapters of Revelation remain. Such a painful year I never passed owing to the privations I have been called to on the one hand, and the spectacle before me of human depravity on the other. But I hope that I have not come to this seat of Satan in vain. The Word of God has found its way into Persia, and it is not in Satan's power to oppose its progress if the Lord has sent it.' By the end of February the New Testament was ready, truly in a marathon timing of eight and a half months. Henry said, 'I have many mercies for which to thank the Lord, and this is not the least. Now may that Spirit who gave the Word, and called me, I trust, to be an interpreter of it, graciously and powerfully apply it to the hearts of sinners, even to the gathering an elect people from amongst the long-estranged Persians' (*A memoir of the Rev Henry Martyn* pp. 410-411). His genius was coupled with humility, and his love for God was reflected in his passion for the Scriptures. With the relief of having the New Testament now ready, he finished the translation of the Book of Psalms in Persian as well. All that remained for him to do now in Shiraz was to supervise the making of several copies of the script of the New Testament. Four copies were sent off at once to his friends at Serampore for printing. As protocol required, the very best scribes in the city were commissioned to prepare two copies, with perfect artistic writing, for the Shah Fath Ali Qajar (r.1797-1834) and his favourite son, Prince Abbas Mirza (1789-1833), his designated heir in the Qajar Dynasty (1785-1925) established by Aqa Mohammed Khan.

Although Henry's health had stabilised since leaving the ferocious heat of the Indian summer, he was still troubled with chest pains, particularly after any long conversation or dispute such as the exhausting debates with the Muslims. There is much of touching interest in many of the conversations with them that he recorded in his journal. They demonstrate not only his faithful witness in declaring the truths of the gospel in the middle of such darkness of unbelief, but also show there was a real seeking after light in the minds of many of his enquirers. The exposition of the Christian message left most angry, but some were eager to know more about Christ the Son of God, the risen Saviour. In the mix of trials and blessings, Henry felt in his declining state an increasing urgency to complete whatever tasks lay ahead in Persia, while realising that the wisest thing to do would be to go straight home to England, if possible to regain his strength and then return to the work in India. He reassured Daniel Corrie in a letter from Persia that he remained strongly attached to that vast and needy country,

Shah Fath Ali Qajar (1771-1834)

which he regarded as his land of adoption.

Interestingly, after their initial dislike of the foreign Christian in their midst, the locals in Shiraz were now reluctant to see him go, inviting him to read stories from the Bible for hours. 'Their love seemed to have increased,' Henry said, as he finally set off from Shiraz on 11 May 1812. He had lived there for nearly a year, and on leaving the Muslim city he found no cause for shaking the dust off his feet. The inhabitants had received, cherished and listened to him, and he departed from them with the blessings and tears of many a Persian friend.

So it was that Henry joined a caravan across the Persian plateau, passing the ruins of ancient Persepolis, the royal city of Darius and Xerxes, which had been burnt down by the soldiers of Alexander the Great in 331 BC. He travelled for twelve days to the magnificent and legendary Safavid city of Isfahan, situated at an altitude of 5,290 feet, and then for another week to the new capital of the old empire, Tehran. He intended to lay the completed translation before the country's ruler, Shah Fath Ali, as it was usual for a Persian writer to present his work to the Shah for his approval before it was published. But his attempt to approach the monarch failed, partly because of the hostility and suspicion of the fanatical populace (eventually, the Muslim monarch was delighted to receive a copy of his New Testament translation, though presented by someone else). Several Muslim scholars called by the antagonistic Shah's Vizier put him under pressure attacking him without courtesy and restraint, and interrupting his replies to their religious challenges and making unfounded assertions. Finally, they summoned him to confess the Islamic Creed. There was a heart-stopping silence before an indignant and impulsive Henry boldly replied, 'There is no God but God and Jesus is the Son of God!' Muslim fury broke loose at this, some asking for his blasphemous tongue to be burnt. His courageous stand and declaration in the middle of open hostility may seem to some to have lacked tact or diplomacy, but Henry could not compromise his responsibility as a true ambassador of Christ.

Prince Abbas Mirza (1789-1833)
As the designated successor to the Persian throne, he was the second person to receive the first copies of Henry's New Testament translation.

His immunity as a foreigner may have spared his life from the aggressive intentions of his opposers, and after advice from friends and reflection on his own part he went north to Tabriz. This city, situated in a valley, was home to an old and important Armenian Christian community, and he hoped to arrange the presentation of his New Testament to the Persian ruler through the good offices of the British ambassador, Sir Gore Ouseley, whom he had met briefly and happily on his arrival in Shiraz. He travelled there from Tehran via the walled city of Zanjan, one of the great trading centres of the Middle East. Somehow he kept on riding despite heavy rain and hail at times; he had little food and his feverish mind began to wander through far happier scenes in India and England. He arrived, more by miracle than anything else, in Tabriz where Prince Abbas Mirza resided as governor of Azerbaijan and Gore Ouseley was staying as a mediator on a complicated diplomatic mission intended to diffuse tense political tensions involving Turkey, Persia and Russia.

---

[19] The portrait painted by W. Hickey was first seen in England in October 1812, and became the possession of Charles Simeon. In 1836, he bequeathed it to Cambridge University Library and it now hangs in the vestry of Holy Trinity Church. There is also a copy of it in St John's College and an engraving after Hickey at the National Portrait Gallery.

6
HIS UNFULFILLED LONGINGS

Return to England: Anticipation and Apprehension

Henry reached the walled city of Tabriz on 7 July 1812 after a debilitating journey of two months on the road in the company of another Englishman in the party which had left Shiraz, Rev. William Canning, who was to take up the position of chaplain at the British Embassy in that city. The emaciated missionary's health was rapidly deteriorating. Lack of sleep and adequate food, exposure to the blaze of the sun and then the cold winds blowing in from the Caspian Sea had drained his strength until he could hardly sit on his horse. One can only wonder how he survived at all. Haggard and dizzy, he was in the grip of his illness and could hardly hold on to life. His cheeks were reddened with a fiery flush but his face was also marked with the morbid look of death. He lay in a raging fever in the ambassador's residence for many days. He was barely conscious, but in lucid moments he was acutely aware of the kind attention he was being given by Gore Ouseley and his wife. He was not far from the threshold of eternity but he could hardly have come to a place better suited to his health. For weeks he lay weak and often delirious, but the constant loving care of his hosts and the congenial climate of Tabriz, 4,200 feet above sea-level, had their effect. In less than two months he was, if not fully restored, at least in better condition. He and Gore Ouseley, an accomplished orientalist with a mastery of a number of eastern languages, found common ground for discussion. The hospitality of the ambassador, his wife and two sons must have been as uplifting and refreshing for Henry as that experienced by those visiting the house of Gaius (see 3 Jn.). He could have enjoyed an extended stay with them but decided against it.

Gore Ouseley and his wife were concerned that Henry should

His unfulfilled longings

contemplate so daunting a prospect of travelling so soon. He would be travelling more than 600 miles across often dangerous country. Kurdish and other bandits were marauding and he would have only a few servants for company. It was something even a robust person would view with apprehension, but they could see their warnings were falling on deaf ears. Henry had become obsessed with the idea of returning to England by the shortest route, even though it was more hazardous than the longer and safer one a sick man would have been advised to take.

As Henry had been unable to meet the Shah in person, the ambassador promised to present his finished work to the Muslim monarch on his behalf. When this was eventually done, the Shah was delighted and publicly expressed his approval,

Tabriz
The place of fleeting recovery

saying it was to be read from beginning to end. (In *The History of the Origin and First Ten Years of the British and Foreign Bible Society* by John Owen, published in 1816, Vol. 1, pp. 265-6, a footnote contains the full text of Fath-Ali Shah's letter to him.) There is no way of knowing whether many Muslims read the New Testament or not, but there is one person we know who definitely did read it. The Scottish Missionary Society report for the year 1822-3 includes news from Darband (Derbent in today's Dagestan), in the Caucasus on the western shore of the Caspian Sea, of the conversion of Mirza Muhammad Ali, the son of a qazi (judge) who was in turn the son of Fath Ali Shah's Prime Minister. The conversion of a Persian Muslim of good birth caused quite a stir; when the missionaries wanted to baptise him, the local Orthodox bishop objected. But they got permission from the Minister of Religion in St Petersburg, and the service was performed by Dr. William Glen. The young man took the name of Alexander Kazen-Beg and was afterwards compelled to enter the Russian civil service and attend the University of Omsk. Kazen-Beg later became a lecturer in Arabic at Kazan University and was one of the founders of oriental studies there. He was later transferred to St Petersburg where he founded, with A.O. Muchlinski, the School of Oriental Studies in the university. The remains of his manuscripts, including his polemical writings in Persian on behalf of Christianity, are preserved in the library there. The invaluable treasure of God's Word in Persian was now to be shared by a multitude of Muslims, and this was indeed the crowning of the sacrificial investment of Henry's precarious life.

Unfortunately, the Shah's Vizier in Tehran did not have the same attitude. Gore Ouseley, however, did yet another great favour for Henry: he took a copy of the Persian New Testament to St Petersburg in 1814, and with the support of the Prince Alexander N. Golitsyn (1773-1844) arranged for the Russian Bible Society to print it, proof-reading it himself.

While still with the Gore Ouseley family, Henry wrote his two final letters to Lydia after he received her last letter in

Shiraz on 14 February 1812. In the first, dated 12 July 1812, a still almost delirious Henry warned her that he might never reach England alive. In the second, dated 28 August, when he was feeling temporarily better, he wrote that he trusted he would shortly see her face to face. With the drawing up of his will, he sent an additional letter to his old long-loved friend and counsellor, Charles Simeon, at Cambridge. He told him of his planned return to England, hoping that he would understand how necessary it was. Henry gave a brief account of his illness and declared that he thought it improbable that he would reach England. He could see the end of his life approaching and wrote, 'Nothing seemingly remains for me to do but to follow the rest of my family to the tomb.' So with very faint hope of ever seeing his native country again, he took to the saddle once more on 2 September 1812. It was the start of his fatal journey north-west through the Persian province of Azerbaijan, and then Armenia and eastern Asia Minor (modern day Turkey). His unconquerable spirit sustained the feeble body for 45 days. He had little pity for himself, undertaking what must have been a nightmare journey, but willing with a sense of despair to endure all the inconveniences involved to get to Constantinople (now Istanbul) first and from there hopefully take a ship via Malta to England. 'If God has work for me to do,' he had written from Shiraz, 'I cannot die.' This was not fatalism or even an irrational optimism, but the inevitable confidence of one who lived close to God whom he knew to be perfect both in wisdom and power (see James 4:15).

It is difficult for us to appreciate now what must have been the acute loneliness of the 18 months Henry spent in Persia, as he faced the fanatical opposition of Islam and the increasing weakness of his body with so few to whom he could turn for sympathy or interest. His solitude would have been almost total if it was not for the consolation of some countrymen and the comfort drawn from God's promises. Yet he was not to leave Persia disillusioned, as he experienced an inner thrill in his soul from the fact that his visit to the country had already

Sir Gore Ouseley (1770-1844)
The British diplomat and his wife were the last compatriots Henry stayed with before proceeding, against their advice, on his fateful journey.

His unfulfilled longings

created a new and unexpected interest in Christianity. In the middle of all the trials he had to endure there were signs that he had not laboured altogether in vain (1 Cor. 15:58; Gal. 6:9). He recorded in his diary his bright hope that the Persians would respond to the gospel in God's own sovereign time (see Is. 55:11). With this blessed assurance as an anchor in his heart, he now knew that he had no more strength to travel to Arabia as he had longed to do in order to search for old Scriptural manuscripts and so perfect the Arabic New Testament. Just as the Apostle Paul appears not to have realised his desire to visit Spain (see Rom. 15:24), so Henry did not fulfil this aspiration.

Equipped with letters of commendation from Gore Ouseley for the Governors of Yerevan, Kars and Erzurum, and for the ambassador at Constantinople, he set out with the support of a small group of servants on an overland journey likely to take two months or more. They rode out of Tabriz at sunset, across a plain towards distant mountains, in a climate which was at its best at this time of year. They followed the royal road of ancient Persia with its mud brick post-stations, shared by men and animals, as they covered about 25 miles a day, often in the night hours to avoid the heat. Ouseley's letters gave Henry a comfortable room in the corners of some mansions in the few established towns and cities on the way, but most stops involved mosquitoes, lice and smelly stables, which sickened him. There was often raucous noise at these places that prevented sleep, and it was frequently left to Henry to get his group up and moving at midnight. They crossed the Araxes, punted over on a rickety old ferry-boat, and rode past Mount Ararat on to the Sultan's domain of Turkey. This meant leaving many Armenians behind who had shown him great kindness and hospitality, to continue a journey which became much less pleasant. Indeed the further his distance from Tabriz, the greater the miseries of his last journey.

After Kars they had a guard from the Pasha to protect them from the Kurds. By 25 September they had reached Erzurum where they stayed three days. They changed their horses and

The city of Yerevan and Mount Ararat with its permanent covering of snow

Yerevan is the capital city of Armenia and was where Henry stayed three days. It has been the coveted object and possession of different peoples down the centuries. The Turks took it from the Persians in 1582 who recovered it in 1604. It was Russian in 1827 and Persian once more from the following year. It fell into the orbit of the Soviet Union until the collapse of communism.

set off again, this time with a powerful Turk, Hassan Aga, joining them. Henry was feeling slightly better, despite a headache, until Hassan made him climb a mountainous track from dawn to dusk and he nearly passed out with the effort. Ignorant of the Turkish language, Henry could not converse with Hassan or the other Turks he met, and was feeling most depressed. Then travellers coming from the opposite direction reported a plague in Constantinople with thousands dying and many of the inhabitants of Tokat, his next destination, fleeing to escape the scourge. Henry realised too late that once again he was passing into imminent danger. He soon found himself subject to the brutality of Hassan, who flogged the baggage-horses until one of them collapsed and claimed the best of any food served to his master, who was too weak to rebuke him. The tough Turk, eager to complete his task as rapidly as possible, had no sympathy at all for Henry's physical weakness. This proved fatal for the invalid, who was susceptible to the cold and damp, and not fit enough to keep up with Hassan's remorseless pace.

The last entries in his journal cover the period from 2 to 6 October. All of them expressed with great lucidity the cross which he had to bear: a merciless and even cruel Hassan. He was 'a thorn in his flesh' as Sabat, the translator, had been to some extent in India.

Journey into Turkey: The Beginning of the End

The journey from Persia into Turkey was perilous and involved great suffering, which Henry could only sustain by the grace of God. His determination to go forth doubled the furnace of fire in his chest and accelerated all the symptoms of his illness. He became even more subject to distress in breathing and suffered a hollow sense of pain and a permanent fatigue. Far away from Tabriz on his way to Tokat, he expressed his thankfulness to the divine Comforter. He made a last note of his private feelings on 6 October 1812: 'I sat in the orchard, and thought with sweet comfort and peace of my God; in solitude my company, my friend, and comforter. Oh! When shall time give place to eternity? When shall appear that new heaven and new earth, wherein dwelleth righteousness?' These were Henry's last recorded words, mentally alert and very devoted to the end. It seems that he used this peaceful interlude in the garden to complete his journal's entries.

The words of the Apostle Paul, a forerunner as torchbearer of the gospel, 'The time of my departure is at hand, I have fought the good fight, I have finished the course, I have kept the faith.' (2 Tim. 4:6, 7), were the answer to a yearning he had expressed previously at Miletus: '… so that I might finish my course with joy, and the ministry, which I have received of the Lord Jesus, to testify the gospel of the grace of God' (Acts 20:24). They may well provide a context for and commentary on Henry's final days on earth. (I would say as a parenthesis that we are reminded here of how Moses led the children of Israel at the beginning of their wilderness journey with a song. Forty years later in Deuteronomy 32 he was still singing, but then, unlike Exodus 15, and despite all the trials which he had endured, he sang alone. Having started the journey with a song, he finished it with a song. It is indeed God 'who gives us songs in the night' (Job. 35:10)). With his high temperature, sweating and shivering, Henry was far too ill thereafter to make any more entries as Hassan dragged him for several more days until the party finally reached Tokat. Henry knew that he could not go further, but a veil of silence descends on his last ten days. For the last time the journal had recorded the thoughts of this dying man with his exasperation and anticipation, and the book was closed only to be opened much later by sorrowing friends in an atmosphere of reverent awe and wonder.

There is something pathetic in the thought of that lonely deathbed in a foreign land. No kinsman was near to watch over him or receive his last words. No close friend stood by his couch to whisper encouragement, close his eyes or wipe the death-sweat from his brow. Those whose privilege it would have been to perform these last offices of love were anxiously expecting tidings of his arrival in England. They knew that he was hastening home with the hope of repairing his shattered body so that he might again devote himself to the work of the Lord in the East. While still in Shiraz in the autumn of 1811 and enjoying the slight recovery he had made there, he thought of hot India: 'the country I have come to regard as my own.' In one of several letters he wrote to Daniel Corrie we read: 'I can conceive of no greater happiness than to settle for life in India superintending schools as we did.' But however lonely Henry's deathbed may have seemed, and whatever yearning thoughts of friends and country may have crossed his mind during those last days, we may be very sure of one thing that 'underneath were the everlasting arms, and the eternal God his refuge' (Deut. 33:27).

Tokat, situated in a fertile valley among granite mountains, was the halfway point on his journey to Constantinople. Attended by two Christians from the substantial Armenian community there, Henry entered into his eternal rest on 16 October 1812. Although his inherited sickness contributed to his death, it is possible that the immediate cause was exhaustion from a fever or even the plague; we cannot be definite from the information available. Whatever the case, far from England and Lydia, he ended his earthly pilgrimage and came into the full joy of a love that has no equal. As is the custom in the East, the body was speedily buried in simple fashion, not in a coffin but in a white winding-sheet.

News travelled more slowly in those days and it was some time before Charles Simeon got to hear of Henry's passing away.

Tokat – 'the portal to eternal glory'

Grieved, he wrote to India to let his friends there know. It was a year of great deprivation for the 53-year-old clergyman as David Brown, another of his devoted friends, passed away after 28 years of service in India. It was on 18 April 1813, six months afterwards, when Daniel Corrie and Thomas Thomason learned what they had always feared since their beloved friend left India on his way to Arabia. Henry's memory remained with them; they revisited places where he had laboured, prompting recollections that were not without emotion. 'During the four years we were fellow-labourers in this country, I had no less than six opportunities of enjoying his company; the last time for four months together, and under the same roof all the time; and each opportunity only increased my admiration for him,' wrote Daniel Corrie who missed his friend for the rest of his life. Henry's missionary labours in Cawnpore, followed up by Corrie there and at Agra soon after, eventually resulted in the baptism of 71 Hindus and Muslims, of whom 50 were adults. All these, save seven, remained steadfast and several became missionaries in their turn.

Lydia was informed about Henry's death on 14 February 1813, ironically, St Valentine's Day! From the contents of a letter dated 14 August 1810, it is clear Henry had a presentiment that he and Lydia were not likely to meet until in the realms of glory although he planned a furlough in England for health reasons. 'It was more than seven years since she had seen him. She wished that she, or some friend, could have been with him at the end. Sometimes she felt he was near, consoling and protecting her, at other times a great sadness overwhelmed her, not least when in later April she had his last letter, written just before he started out from Tabriz' (*My Love Must Wait; the story of Henry Martyn* p. 154).

If only Henry had been granted the consolation of an engagement before he died as his hero David Brainerd was with his very young and beloved Jerusha,[20] daughter of the outstanding preacher Jonathan Edwards (1703-1758) and compiler of his writings, that might have been a balm for the afflictions of the dying lover. Eight years had passed since the first occasion Henry had met Lydia as an adult in the summer of 1804; years of delightful expectations and dreams mixed with the painful fear that they were but a chimera.

Lydia, freed at last from confronting a decision with which she had seemed unable to cope, continued to live for a further 17 years, somewhat like a widow quietly mourning the memory of the man she had loved. 'Many waters cannot quench love nor can the floods drown it' (Song of Solomon 8:7). In the last three years of her life, she was tragically afflicted by a mental disorder requiring temporary asylum, and had breast cancer. She died on 21 September 1829 at the age of 54 in Henry's sister's house, the old vicarage of Breage in Cornwall. It seems likely his memory dominated her thoughts or at least was cherished as her diary records: 16 October 1820[21] – 'I have now survived my beloved friend eight years,' 11 January 1823 – 'Placed in my room yesterday the print of dear Martyn' and 18 June 1826 (her last entry) – 'beloved Henry.' It is well said, 'genuine love never dies, it is eternal' for 'love is as strong as death' (Song of Solomon 8:6).

---

[20] There is a disagreement among historians and biographers about their being betrothed. Thomas Brainerd, who was in possession of the original diaries of David and John Brainerd, had no doubt they were engaged. Richard Ellsworth Day (*Flagellant on Horseback*, 1950) and David Wynbeek (*Beloved Yankee*, 1961) take the same view. Yet, the fact that there is no mention of it in Jonathan Edwards' original publication has led to an ongoing debate. The late Rev. David D. Field, author of *The Genealogy of the Brainerd Family in the United States*, says, 'They had anticipated great happiness in married life in this world …' (p. 283).

[21] Erratum: The brilliant historian, Stephen Neill, erroneously writes that he dies in Persia in 1813 in *A History of Christian Missions*, p 266.

7
THE IMPACT OF HIS LIFE

Institutional Memorials

In his six years of labour in foreign lands, Henry had indeed 'burned out for God.' At the beginning, he probably had little idea how fast the blaze of that inner fire would consume him. Alone he stood his ground in unshaken and triumphant faith where most would have given up. Truly he could have said like the Apostle Paul, 'I have fought the good fight, I have finished the race, I have kept the faith' (2 Tim. 4:7).[22]

Henry was hastily buried by some Armenians in the extensive Armenian cemetery at Tokat. Afterwards, when some concerned Christians searched out his resting-place they were shocked by the sight and felt obliged to re-inter his remains in a more becoming way. Then under the auspices of the East India Company's representative in Baghdad, Claudius James Rich (1787-1821), a proper limestone slab was placed on the tomb with the following words inscribed in Latin:

'A PIOUS AND FAITHFUL SERVANT,
Sacerdos ac Missionarius Anglorum,
called by the Lord Himself,
as he was returning to his fatherland.'

When Dr. Henry van Lennep went to live in the city as a missionary in 1854 he found the site in a decaying state. Henry's bodily remains were removed and laid in the first grave of the newly-opened missionary cemetery of the Presbyterian American Mission. The Board of Directors of the East India Company funded the erection of a pyramidal obelisk in local marble with the same epitaph on each side of its four-square base, written in English, Armenian, Turkish and Persian with the following inscription:

> Rev. Henry Martyn, M.A.
> Chaplain of the Hon. East India Company,
> Born at Truro, England, February 18, 1781
> Died at Tokat, October 16, 1812.
> He laboured for many years in the East, striving to benefit mankind both in this world and that to come. He translated the Holy Scriptures into Hindustani and Persian, and preached the God and Saviour of Whom they testify. He will long be remembered in the East, where he was known as a Man of God.

The memorial was shaded by weeping willow trees, the only specimens in the region, planted by a number of admirers including the biographer George Smith (*Henry Martyn: Saint and Scholar* p. 530). The grave stood upon a broad and high terrace, overlooking the town, but then vanished with the vicissitudes of time. The author tried to investigate its whereabouts, but as the Australian biographer, Marcus Loane, had written, 'During a visit to Tokat in September 1968 I found that the site of Henry Martyn's grave cannot now be identified; the land has been resumed as a site for a school. But the obelisk has been rescued and placed in a local museum opposite the old missionary cemetery. The name has been defaced from all four sides, but the English inscription at the base is still clear. Thus his grave, like that of Moses, is now unknown; but he was a burning and a shining light in his own generation. That light went out when he died' (*Henry Martyn: a Star in the Orient* in *They Were Pilgrims* p. 95). But his testimony did speak and still speaks.

When the news of Henry's death arrived in England, Parliament was discussing the missionary clauses of the East India Company's charter. The tidings became a catalyst for opening up unrestricted opportunities for the preaching of the gospel in India. 1813 became an important year for the free evangelisation of this large nation and the beginning of a great missionary advance in other parts of the world. These had been

*The memorial at Tokat funded by
the East India Company*

deprived too long of the knowledge of true pardon, eternal salvation and reconciliation to God, and the message began to be made available to sinners through the proclamation of the gospel in its simple and clear presentation of a risen Lord and a living Saviour called Jesus! (see Acts 4:14; 1 Tim. 2:4-6).

A phenomenon in his time, several institutions or foundations across the world uphold Henry's legacy to the present time. Among these is the beautiful cathedral in Truro, consecrated in 1887 where visitors can see his life depicted in eight stained glass windows around the walls of the baptistery, a notable achievement for Truro's eminent son.

At Cambridge University a hall was named after him in 1887. Hyderabad in India has a Henry Martyn Institute of Islamic Studies, and there was a Henry Martyn Academy (now called the International Gateway Academy) for schooling foreign Christian children in Istanbul in Turkey.

Above all his achievements, Henry was a man longing for God; always striving to enter more deeply into every Christian experience, thirsting after righteousness, critical of his own weaknesses and deploring what he felt to be a lack of holy living. For him as for the renowned evangelist, John Wesley, God's work in them was far more important than their work for Him. It was their desire to practise a living Christian confession rather than be satisfied with mere profession. Neither man was spared the calumnies and envy of their countrymen and others, and had to learn in a spirit of piety, verity, charity and purity to cope with this. Sad to say, there will always be those like Diotrephes: 'prating against us with malicious words' (see 3 Jn. 9, 10).

Written Records

Before Henry left India, he wanted to burn all his private papers but refrained from doing so. He agreed instead to seal them up and leave them with his trusted and dear friend Daniel Corrie in Cawnpore. This packet was opened after his death and was found to contain all his journals from 1803 to 1810. All his later writings were among the papers that were entrusted to his loyal Armenian servant, Sergius. He in turn gave the material to Isaac Morier, the British Consul in Constantinople, who conveyed the papers to Henry's close acquaintances in England. Charles Simeon and John Sargent pored over these travel-worn documents, and they formed the basis for the memoir lovingly compiled by Sargent. This was published in 1819, and went through ten editions before his death in 1833. But he suppressed the bulk of the material which had to do with Lydia Grenfell as she was still alive, and it fell to his son-in-law, Samuel Wilberforce, to bring out a separate edition of the journals and letters in two volumes in 1837.[23] Henry's entries in his journals had been made in private and were clearly modelled on the pattern of David Brainerd's diary, to which he owed so much. They were meant for one pair of eyes only for they told the story of one who tried to walk with God and were written with a pensive frankness that was only possible because he wrote them as though he were in the very presence of God.

Few books apart from the Psalms of David reflect as much of the hidden longing in a believer's heart for perfect conformity to the divine purpose as do Henry's journals. It is in fact a book which throbs with the hunger of a soul that must feed on Christ or die. He recorded in black and white that which he had learned in solitude and trials, and it was in anguish of soul that he produced writings of unselfconscious beauty. Bishop Stephen Neill has described it as 'one of the most precious treasures of Anglican devotion' (Stephen Neill, *A History of Christian Missions*, p. 267).

A few additional extracts from his diary will suffice to show the reality of his longing for total dependence on God to grow and be used, and the enjoyment of deep communion with Him by means of the Word and prayer. He wrote when aboard ship en route to India:

My mind, this morning, easily ascended to God in peaceful solemnity: I succeeded in finding access to God, and being alone with Him: Could I but enjoy this life of faith more steadily, how much should 'I grow in grace,' and be renewed in the spirit of my mind. At such seasons of fellowship with the Father and His Son Jesus Christ, when the world, and self, and eternity, are nearly in the right places, not only are my views of duty clear and comprehensive, but the proper motives have a more constraining influence … I came to my rooms rejoicing to be alone again, and to hold communion with God. … Read Isaiah the rest of the evening, sometimes happy, but at other times tired, and desiring to take up some other religious book; but I saw it an important duty to check this slighting of the Word of God. … Endeavoured to consider what should be my study and preparation for the mission; but could devise no particular plan, but to search the Scriptures: What are God's promises respecting the spread of the Gospel, and the means by which it shall be accomplished? Long seasons of prayer in behalf of the heathen, I am sure, are necessary (Is. 62). Began Isaiah, and learned by heart the promises scattered through the first twelve chapters hoping that they may prove profitable matter for meditation as well as prayer. … My whole soul wrestled with God: I knew not how to leave off crying to Him to fulfil His promises; chiefly pleading His own glorious power: I do not know that anything would be a Heaven to me, but the service of Christ and the enjoyment of His presence: O how sweet is life, when spent in His service! I am going upon a work exactly according to the mind of Christ; and my glorious Lord, Whose power is uncontrollable, can easily open the way for His feeble follower, through the thickest of the ranks of His enemies: And now, on let me go, smiling at my foes; how small are human obstacles, before this mighty Lord! How easy is it for God to effect His purposes in a moment! What are inveterate prejudices, when once the Lord shall set to His hand! In prayer I had a most precious view of Christ, as a Friend that sticketh closer than a brother. Oh, how sweet was it to pray to Him! I hardly knew how to contemplate with praise enough His adorable excellencies. Who can show forth all His praise!

After arriving in India, his diary records his continued aspirations after God:

> How sweet is prayer to my soul at this time: I seem as if I could never be tired, not only of spiritual joys, but of spiritual employments, since these are now the same. ... I felt as if I could never be tired of prayer. ... At night read the third and fourth chapters of the Acts; and lost much time and spirituality by indulging ideas of schemes about the Gospel, which had more of romance and pride in them than a wisdom and humiliation. ... What a source of perpetual delight have I in the precious Book of God! O that my heart were more spiritual, to keep pace with my understanding; and that I could feel as I know: May my root and foundation be deep in love, and may I be able to 'comprehend, with all saints, what is the breadth, and length, and depth, and height, and to know the love of Christ which passeth knowledge!' And may I be filled with all the fullness of God! May the Lord, in mercy to my soul, save me from setting up an idol of any sort in His place; as I do by preferring even a work professedly done by Him, to communion with Him. How obstinate is the reluctance of the natural heart to love God! But, O my soul, be not deceived; thy chief work upon earth is to obtain sanctification, and to walk with God: 'To obey is better than sacrifice, and to hearken than the fat of rams.' Let me learn from this that to follow the direct injunctions of God, as to my own soul, is more my duty than to be engaged in other works, under the pretence of doing Him service. ... The determination with which I went to bed last night, of

devoting this day to prayer and fasting, I was enabled to put into execution: In my first prayer for deliverance from worldly thoughts, depending on the power and promises of God, for fixing my soul while I prayed, I was helped to enjoy much abstinence from the world for nearly an hour: Then read the history of Abraham, to see how familiarly God had revealed Himself to mortal men of old: Afterward, in prayer for my own sanctification, my soul breathed freely and ardently after the holiness of God, and this was the best season of the day.

Of his native assistant in translating the New Testament, he wrote: 'Sabat lives almost without prayer, and this is sufficient to account for all evils that appear in saint or sinner.'

Burden and Vision

Let us remember that it was Henry's early desire that his example would cause others to catch his vision and take up the burden, even if his own efforts proved sterile. The number of those inspired by his pioneering work and early death to live and die that Christ might be revealed to Muslims may not be as great as the thousands who have been spiritually stimulated by his journals, but his prayer has been answered and there have been many who became recipients and channels of God's blessings to the lost around the world.

Those influenced by the reading of his life include Reginald Heber (1783-1826), best known for his hymn of adoration, 'Holy, Holy, Holy, Lord God Almighty,' and the missionary hymn, 'From Greenland's Icy Mountains,' the last stanza of which has such a stirring appeal to Christian hearts:

> Shall we, whose souls are lighted
> With wisdom from on high,
> Shall we to men benighted
> The lamp of life deny?

Salvation! O salvation!
The joyful sound proclaim,
Till earth's remotest nation
Has learned Messiah's name.

Henry's heroic labours had so kindled within Reginald Heber an inextinguishable flame that he followed in his footsteps to Calcutta in 1823. From there, he began a ministry which encompassed the whole of India, Ceylon (Sri Lanka) and most of the south Pacific. In a zealous missionary service, which lasted only three years in a difficult tropical climate and trying conditions, Heber witnessed a spiritual breakthrough among some of the natives, especially the Tamils, which Henry did not have the privilege of seeing. Interestingly, it was Reginald Heber as bishop who ordained Abdul Masih as an Anglican clergyman in 1825 at Calcutta, and this in the presence of Daniel Corrie.

William J Jowett was another well-known 19th century missionary who found great inspiration in reading what was available on Henry's life. He laboured in Syria and Palestine from 1815 to 1830, and wrote later, reflecting on his consecration, 'I think of Henry Martyn, that brilliant Cambridge wrangler, grasping the coveted honours of his beloved university, and yet strangely hungry in the hour of his academic triumph: "I was surprised to find that I had grasped a shadow." Oh, but it was a surprise of grace, a blessed disappointment, inspired by the Holy Spirit. "The Spirit of the Lord bloweth upon it," and the coveted glory fades like the withered grass. It was a gracious disillusionment, for Henry Martyn's eyes were now lifted far above scholastic prizes to the all-satisfying "prize of the high calling of God in Christ Jesus our Lord." Having gazed upon the glory of the Lord, his eyes were washed to discern the vastness of the Lord's untilled and fruitless fields, and he turned his consecrated life to India' (William MacDonald, *Grasping the shadows* p. 12).

Among many other outstanding pioneer-missionaries to

the East, Anthony N. Groves (1795-1853) – sometimes called the 'father of faith missions' – comes to mind. He was so enthralled by Henry's example that he gave up a lucrative dentistry practice at the age of 34 and followed in his wake with his family and a small band of workers. He was marked by the same spirit of complete abandonment to the Lord, firstly in a trying and somewhat unsuccessful four-year missionary enterprise in Baghdad. Learning Arabic to reach the Muslims, Groves was

Anthony N. Groves (1795-1853)
Chain reactions. Henry was a major influence on this man – sometimes called the 'father of faith missions' – who went out to do Christian work in the East in full dependence on and obedience to the Lord. He, in turn, inspired such people as his son-in-law, George Muller (1806-1898), who established a large orphanage in Bristol supported by direct answers to prayer.[24]

frustrated but not defeated by various oppositions and calamities. Tribulations and deprivations such as plague – he lost his wife and small daughter to typhus – robbers and so on marked the heroic career of a man who would not give up the cause of Christ in heathen lands! After the failed attempt to establish a work in Mesopotamia (today's Iraq), he went to India where his 20-year service proved more fruitful. All these missionary efforts were characterised by total dependence on God's promises to supply and sustain, and loyal obedience to the Lord Jesus and a faithful adherence to the injunctions of His Word. On his adventurous and perilous journey to the mission field across Russia, the Caucasus and Persia in 1829, he wrote: 'I never had very strong expectation of what we were to do being manifestly very great, but that we shall answer a purpose in God's plans I have no doubt' (George H Lang, *Anthony Norris Groves, saint and pioneer: a combined study of a man of God and of the original principles of the Brethren* p.186). His example has had a growing influence from the time he left his native England to launch into 'deep waters' in confident and triumphant faith. Groves was instrumental in bringing a fresh stimulus to the Lord's work in the regions beyond, and until this day his legacy has a worldwide imprint on the Brethren missionary movement, which is not inclined to flashy publicity but strives for spiritual integrity in the presentation of its efforts and results – all to the glory of God.

Beside Reginald Heber, William Jowett and Anthony Groves, a train of later missionaries, unsung heroes of the cross, followed Henry, like Ian Keith 'Falconer of Arabia' (1856-1887), Valpy French of India (1825-1891) and Robert Bruce of Persia (1833 -1915). The list could be extended to include many more who were not hesitant to say they looked at and were electrified by some of the features of Henry's life and service and sought to emulate them. No doubt, a new generation of Christians can do the same as his memory is revived and used by the Spirit of God to shape them for the Lord's service whether as witnesses at home or abroad.

Henry laid down his life prematurely just like his hero David Brainerd, who had an irresistible appeal for him and drew out the depths of his admiration. When most men are starting their life's work, Henry had finished his. He had the merit of having translated the New Testament into three important Muslim languages of Arabic script but refused to be praised. 'Praise is exceedingly unpleasant to me,' he wrote when listeners praised his sermons at Cambridge. He would not want a glowing record of his virtues and achievements. He attributed all these to God alone! He has left us an example, not of a perfect man, but of what God can do with a very imperfect man who takes Him seriously. As Richard T. France wrote in his narrative: 'Who has not known times when he was afraid to speak in the cause of Christ ? So did Martyn, and rebuked himself for his fear of man, but it was with him to the end, a fear usually conquered, but nevertheless truly fought. Who has not said and done things he would give anything to recall? So did the impetuous Martyn. Who has not known his love for God dimmed by too great a love for the pleasures of the world, or gone through long periods of spiritual barrenness, when all joy in religion seemed impossible, God seemed far off, and doubts arose incessantly? So did Martyn, and cried out in despair. No one was more keenly aware of his weakness than Martyn himself, whose diary some have labelled morbid, but which bears rather the stamp of a stark realism' (*Five Pioneer Missionaries* pp. 296-297).

Following criticisms by some early readers bored by some of Henry's private writings, John Sargent wrote in the preface to the tenth issue of his editorial work (published by Seeley & Co in 1862) that he was anxious to remove a misconceived impression which seemed to have got abroad that Henry was of a gloomy disposition and lacking in human sympathy. He disowned this view, which some share even today, and assured his readers from personal testimony, 'that Henry Martyn was not less cheerful as a companion than he was warm-hearted as a friend.' The erroneous conception, which Sargent deplored, was unquestionably due to readers of the letters and journals taking Henry at his own estimate and accepting his expressions of self-depreciation to which he constantly gave way as literally true. Henry's legacy may also be found in the secular world. In the literary forum, there has been a theory supported recently by Valentine Cunningham, Fellow in English at Corpus Christi College, Oxford, that St. John Rivers in the classic novel *Jane Eyre* by Charlotte Brontë (1816-1855) is based on his life, if not his character. Henry had helped Brontë's father, then known as Patrick Brunty, when he was a young student at St. John's College, and was, it is said, his hero.

Intellectual Achievements

The original copy of Henry's New Testament in Persian was published in 1815 in St. Petersburg by the Russian Bible Society.[25] The second edition was published by the Mission Press in Serampore, and Said Ali of Shiraz was invited to Calcutta in 1816 to supervise the printing. (The Old Testament translation was undertaken by Dr. William Glen, the Scottish missionary, and published in 1846, three years before his passing away in Tehran at the age of 71.) In 1880, Robert Bruce, the Irish missionary, based in nearby Isfahan, was commissioned to make a revision of the whole Persian Bible, and this was printed in 1895 at Leipzig, Germany. Since then other linguists have worked to improve the text, and a new translation of the New Testament was published in London in the summer of 2003, (coinciding with the release of the German version of this book) after seven years' hard work by a team of 25 people. This is expected to replace the current standard Persian translation, which is over 100 years old and difficult for many people, especially younger readers, to understand. There was a great need for this translation, given that over 60% of Iran's 70 million people are under the age of 21.[26]

The Arabic New Testament translated by Nathaniel Sabat under Henry's supervision, was also printed in Calcutta in

*Dr. Glen's memorial stone in
the old Armenian church in Tehran*

1816.²⁷ In his personal evaluation of Henry's linguistic gifts, John Malcolm, the British diplomat, declared: 'His knowledge of Arabic is superior to that of any Englishman in India' (John Kaye, W. *The life and correspondence of Major-General Sir John Malcolm* Vol. 2, p. 65).

This translation has now been long superseded, but it was the first separate New Testament text in Arabic for almost half a century. Meanwhile, in 1814, the Mission Press in Serampore published the Urdu New Testament, which Henry had translated. Undoubtedly this New Testament was his greatest single work, and has been largely used in all subsequent revisions (a much needed revision was made in 2003). It was so highly regarded linguistically that it was set as a textbook in Muslim schools in Agra. The version in use today is clearly a descendant of this. (It was Thomas Thomason who supervised the Old Testament translation into Urdu.)

It is difficult to fully comprehend the size and complexity of the task Henry faced in accurately communicating the truth in eastern idioms and languages foreign to such terms as grace, redemption, church and so on. Kenneth Cragg, a contemporary scholarly interpreter of the Christian faith to Muslims, and of Islam to Christians, has written in *Troubled by Truth: Life-Studies in Inter-Faith Concern* (1992): 'Martyn's brief career in missionary translation is as telling as any concerning the problematics of words and terms in the transactions of faith. Martyn encountered the ... situation and faced it with a strong equipment of scholarship sustained by steady anguish of spirit. ... It is evident in Martyn how he was more vitally in encounter with theology-in-philology than any academic professor. For he was made to feel, via his [able native collaborators], the full strain, and even the venom, of the resistance to meaning implicit in the otherness of words.'

Besides these translations in Arabic script, Henry wrote a series of tracts in Persian replying to the apologetic work on Islam by Mirza Ibrahim who raised several arguments against Christianity. In the controversy, he showed his knowledge of the religious mind of Islam and his acquaintance with the Koran, and his characteristic courtesy in dealing with Muslims (see 2 Tim. 2:24,25). Some of these tracts were published in 1824 by Samuel Lee, Professor of Arabic at Cambridge but, for all their merit, they have been superseded by more erudite works.

Henry's way of dealing with the claims of Islam differed from some of his important Protestant successors as missionaries to Muslims. 'While he was willing to enter into debate with Muslim leaders and scholars, to subject the conflicting claims of Christianity and Islam to public discussion, he was somewhat cautious about the usefulness of this approach and he set himself one important rule in debate, never to attack Islam publicly.' (Hugh Goddard, *A history of Christian-Muslim relations* p. 123). Subsequent events show clearly the wisdom of

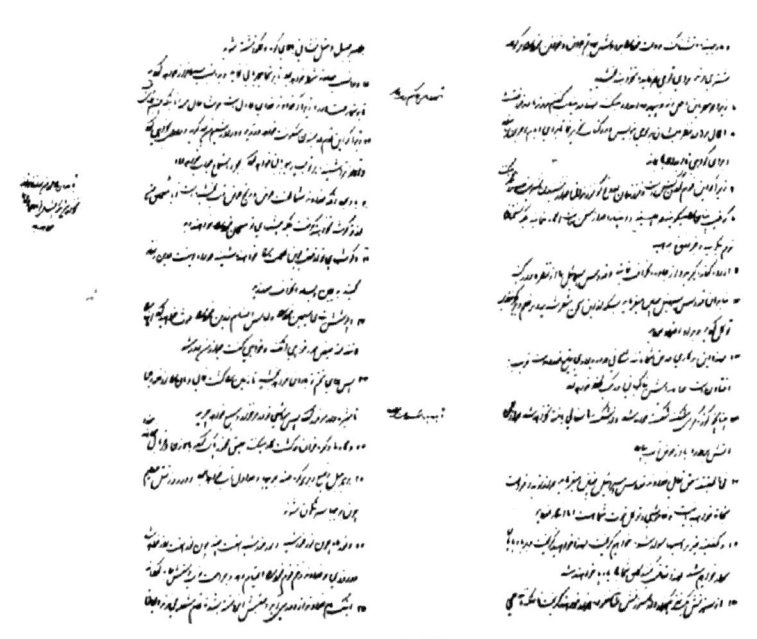

Memorabilia
One of Henry's most precious possessions still in existence is a number of volumes of his manuscript Persian New Testament, now in the archives of the CMS. These valuable documents were originally purchased at a second-hand book shop in Birmingham with no explanation of how they arrived there.

this approach (see Joseph S. & Pillsbury B. L. K. (eds.) *Muslim-Christian Conflicts* Boulder (CO): Westview Press, 1978). He wrote to Charles Simeon from Tabriz to warn his friends in Cambridge against a precipitate move to publish a work for Muslim readers, stressing the need for input from men who were experts in understanding eastern ways. But while he evidently believed it was important to consider the cultural context and characteristics of people in presenting the gospel to them, he was not a precursor of those who advocate the use of anthropology and ethnology at the expense of sound biblical theology and the unambiguous declaration of the universal truths of Holy Scripture. There is a dangerous trend in our days towards a pragmatism in preaching the gospel which tends to betray its dogmatic truths for the sake of quick results. This is of real concern for those who want to stay faithful to biblical Christianity (see my book *Muslims Near and Far Away – Challenges and Opportunities*).

Henry's personal evangelism among Muslims was a new feature and he proved to be at his best when quietly sharing his experiences of Christ with them in a small circle of interested listeners. These intimate talks, sometimes with individuals, tended to produce a mutual response: 'A new impression was left on my mind; namely that these men are not fools and that all ingenuity and clearness of reasoning are not confined to England and Europe ... I find that seriousness in the declaration of the truths of the Gospel is likely to have more power than the clearest argument conveyed in a trifling spirit' (*A memoir of the Rev Henry Martyn* pp. 198, 243). 'Thus, Martyn by his questions and contribution to apologetics and personal evangelism, set the pace for the missionary movement to Muslims' (Lyle L Vander Werff, *Christian mission to Muslims: the record* p.36).

As a scholar and controversialist Henry found a worthy successor in the German missionary in Persia and India, Karl Gottlieb Pfander (1803-1865), though he had a contrasting personality and was certainly more abrasive in his approach to Muslims. In 1835, he published his famous apologetic book *Balance of Truth* in Persian, a brilliant treatise which sets out the supreme validity of Christianity in contrast to the claims of Islam.[28] In this and other literary works, Pfander quotes from Henry's tracts. While public reaction forced him to flee for his life from Persia and Arabia, God used these and the repercussions of his public debates at Agra in northern India, to bring several prominent Muslims to acknowledge Christ as the Son of the Living God and their personal Saviour. They in

Karl G. Pfander (1803-1865)
*Karl G Pfander was as robust in his writings
as he was in his public discourses in the East.*

their turn entered into the Christian ministry with resounding impact. *The Balance of Truth* has survived the tumult it provoked among Muslims at the time and, interestingly, some converts from Islam today find this controversial study of great value.

Testimony and Tribute

Henry's exemplary life was as convincing as his arguments. He endured abuses and threats with equanimity and mostly treated all with courtesy. For instance a certain Mohammed Rahim who was gradually persuaded of the truth of Henry's teaching, told him of his conviction when the missionary was just about to leave Shiraz. Henry gave Rahim a Persian New Testament which he often read. On one of the first blank pages of the book was written: 'There is joy in heaven over one sinner that repenteth. Henry Martyn.' Rahim has left us his impression of Henry's stay in Shiraz: 'In the year 1223 of the Hegira [Muslim calendar], came to this city an Englishman, who taught the religion of Christ with a boldness hitherto unparalleled in Persia, in the midst of much scorn and ill treatment from our religious leaders, as well as from the common people. He was a pale youth, and evidently enfeebled by disease. I was then a decided enemy to infidels [Christians], and visited the teacher of the despised sect with the declared object of treating him with scorn and exposing his doctrines to contempt. These evil feelings gradually subsided under the influence of his gentleness, and just before he quitted Shiraz, I paid a farewell visit. Our conversation – the recollection of it will never fade from the tablets of my memory – sealed my conversion. He gave me a book; it has been my constant companion; the study of it has formed my most delightful occupation' (*Henry Martyn: Saint and Scholar* pp. 525-526, paraphrased).

In reading the account above of the polarisation and tension which Henry and other Christian witnesses encounter in presenting the claims of Christ, the Son of God, as the risen Saviour of the world, the words of the Apostle Peter have timeless weight and import, as the case of Mohammed Rahim shows: 'Beloved, I beg you as sojourners and pilgrims, abstain from fleshly lusts which war against the soul, having your conduct honourable among the Gentiles, that when they speak against you as evildoers, they may, by your good works which they observe, glorify God in the day of visitation … For this is the will of God, that by doing good you may put to silence the ignorance of foolish men' *(1 Pet. 2:11-12, 15).*

John McNeill (1795-1883) came to Persia in 1821 as an assistant surgeon to the British delegation in Tehran. After 15 years there he became one of the most capable and influential diplomats in Persia (1836-1842) and one of the very few British officials to gain the high esteem of the Qajar court, which did not give praise lightly. He wrote from Tabriz in 1825, 'Henry Martyn produced in Persia a greater impression than any other man could now hope to do, for he not only admirably calculated for the understanding, but he was perhaps the first Christian divine who showed himself superior to the Persians in all the learning on which they most valued themselves ... he elicited a spirit of enquiry and discussion which had not existed before his time, and he taught the Persians to respect a religion that instilled in its votaries the lofty principles of virtue and benevolence which they admired in him' *(The English amongst the Persians during the Qajar period, 1787-1921* p. 114). In the eyes of the Persians, Henry's deportment was in sharp contrast to the vanity and arrogance of British and other foreign officials. John Malcolm and most of his successors often used their position of superiority to humiliate people they regarded as their inferiors, sometimes making abusive demands, and at intervals courting them as allies and betraying them as rivals in their quest for global power and influence. Henry, for his part, had that nobility and integrity which friends and foes acknowledged, a combination too often lacking in those with political, military and economic power, whatever their nationality (see Rev. 14:13; Prov. 10:7).

Following Henry's route, the freelance itinerant Christian literature distributor, Peter Gordon, a former sea-captain, passed through Isfahan where he was impressed to hear such positive memories of his predecessor from the mouths of Muslims (see *Fragment of the Journal of a Tour Through Persia in 1820*). Joseph Wolff (born 1796), a German Jewish convert who also came under the benign influence of Charles Simeon, went to the Middle East to witness to both Jews and Muslims. While he was in Tehran in 1830, he happened to meet the mullahs who vividly remembered their controversy with the solitary but valiant Henry who stood in peril of his life for what he believed. To some of his generation, Henry's passage through their lives was more than meteoric.

All his life Henry was dependant upon the Holy Spirit to open ears and hearts to receive the message of salvation: 'In your prayers for me pray that utterance may be given that I may open my mouth boldly to make known the mysteries of the Gospel. I often envy my Persian hearers the freedom and eloquence with which they speak to me. Were I but possessed of their powers I sometimes think that I should win them all; but the work is God's and the faith of his people does not stand in the wisdom of men, but in the power of God' (*Henry Martyn: Saint and Scholar* p. 364). He knew the value of an intellectual approach to the Muslims but it never became a substitute for the divine intervention of the Holy Spirit, and that led him to confess: 'I never felt so strongly that I can do nothing. All my clear arguments are useless; unless the Lord stretches out His hand, I speak to stones.'

By preaching the gospel to the ignorant, and causing languages to speak to the heart and conscience of those glorious truths of the gospel of which they had hitherto been dumb, he made the oracles of God accessible to millions and became a channel of blessing, the extent of which will not be known until time is no more. As has been well said: 'when only twenty-seven years of age Henry Martyn inaugurated a new era of Christian witness to the Muslims. For his undying fame rests on his translation of the New Testament into Urdu and Persian, whereby he laid the foundation of all subsequent work among the Muslims. It was from this time that translations of the Bible into the languages of the Muslim world were, at intervals, undertaken and completed' (*People of the mosque* p. 241). So it was that the first complete Urdu Bible became available in 1843, followed by the Persian in 1846 and the Arabic in 1865.

Today there are vibrant Christian gatherings in Pakistan and northern India from Punjab to Bihar where Urdu is spoken, as well as in Iran. While Henry embraced God's promises by faith for a coming harvest in these parts of the Muslim world, his successors became partakers of it and the joyful reapers of its fruits (see 1 Cor. 15:58; Gal. 6:9). This remarkable individual could see beyond the horizons of time and 'endured as seeing Him who is invisible' (Heb. 11:27). In his day, Henry saw Persia as a 'field ripe for the harvest. Vast numbers secretly hate and despise the superstition imposed on them, and as many of them as have heard the Gospel, approve it; but they dare not hazard their lives for the name of the Lord Jesus.' And he definitely saw his Persian New Testament as a spiritual breakthrough for the advancement of God's purpose among the Muslims.

As the late Miss Constance Padwick wrote in her popular and well-written account of 1922: 'His life still speaks to the world with a message as vital and urgent as that proclaimed by his own lips or pen. He belongs to that band of missionary saints, devoured by a consuming zeal, which gave them no rest, but drove them ever onwards to greater endeavours for the furtherance of the kingdom of God. It was the constraining love of Christ, and the vision of souls eternally lost, which led Henry Martyn to the shores of India. But until his journals were read after his death, few realised how strong was that constraining power, how clear that vision, or how careful had been his preparation for His Master's service' (*Henry Martyn: Confessor of the Faith*, p. 168). Let us conclude with the final appraisal of George Smith in his monumental biography: 'We live in hurrying times; our days are swifter than a shuttle. New names, new saints, new heroes ever rise and dazzle the eyes of common men. So it should be, for God lives, and through Him men live and manifest His unexhausted power. But Martyn is a perennial. He springs up fresh to every generation' (*Henry Martyn: Saint and Scholar*, p. 490).

***An illustration by the Musavvir ul Mulk of
the raising by Jesus of the widow's son at Nain***

Though most Iranian Muslims are great devotees of their rich culture, they are not always aware that the well-known artists they admire often referred to Christ in their works. The two couplets in the illustration above are taken from the third book *of the Mathnavi of Jalalu'ddin Rumi, the greatest of the Persian mystical poets of the 13th century, and clearly refer to the story in Lk. 7:11-16. The couplets may be rendered:*

'Oh, do not deem the words of Christ mere sound and breath, But note there fled away from Him the spectre of Death! Deem not His accent rough, His style inerudite, See how the dead man leapt to life and sat upright!'

A more recent example was Husayn Behzad who died in 1968. He was a convert to Christianity, but was denied a Christian funeral and given a large official Muslim burial ceremony in Tehran instead.[29] However, some Muslims are willing to examine the roots or source of their religion, especially in places where Christianity once flourished such as Kabylia in Algeria. A fresh presentation of the gospel in their own languages is vital for such if they are to be fully enlightened and see the glory of God in the face of Jesus Christ.

---

[22] Here I am reminded of someone else who was ready to live a short but worthwhile life without regret. When John Tornquist – a missionary in Eastern Turkestan from 1904 – addressed a group of young people in Sweden in 1919, he said, 'If I were to start my life all over again, I would have no greater ambition than to be a missionary.' In 1935, two years before his death, he wrote in his diary on the way out to the field, 'If God the Father suddenly spoke to me in a human voice and said, "You have thirty years to live on earth, provided you stay in Europe. If, however, you prefer to go to Asia, you will only have ten years," I would then gladly accept the ten years and continue on my journey to the field' (Hultvall, John *Mission och Revolution i Centralasien* Stockholm: Gummessons, 1981, p. 156).

[23] Unfortunately, the original journals, the most valuable source of all for a knowledge of Henry Martyn's life, seem to have disappeared. Most of the material was committed to Daniel Corrie in India and sent by him to Henry's executors, Charles Simeon and John Thornton, in 1814. The latter part of the journals came into the hands of Isaac Morier in Constantinople and was sent by him to Simeon's rooms at Cambridge about that time. John Sargent referred to it for his biography and Samuel Wilberforce had access to it in 1837, but there the

trail disappears. Dr. George Smith never alludes to the original journals in his exhaustive work in 1892; all his quotations are derived from Sargent and Wilberforce. He could not go behind them, and neither can we today. Exhaustive enquiries have not yielded the slightest clue to their whereabouts. They may have been destroyed after the publication of Wilberforce's extracts. If they were to be found, it is likely a further biography of Henry would become necessary. We could draw from them what Sargent and Wilberforce, with their now distant viewpoints, did not think worth elaborating. In spite of the shortness of Henry's life and the disappearance of his journals, his biographers are all faced with the task of summarising many thousands of pages of information by him and about him. *The Journals and Letters of the Rev. Henry Martyn* in two volumes, edited by Samuel Wilberforce and published after Lydia Grenfell's death, reveal more than was thought desirable when John Sargent wrote his *A Memoir of the Reverend Henry Martyn* (cf. Bentley-Taylor, pp. 159-160).

[24] Others influenced by Groves include the founders of missionary enterprises such as the North Africa Mission (called Arab World Ministries today) inaugurated by George Pearce (1814-1902), and the China Inland Mission (called The Overseas Missionary Fellowship today) founded by Hudson Taylor (1832-1905) whose motto 'God's work, done in God's way, will never lack God's supply' has proved of great blessing to a multitude of Christians who have learned to look only to the Lord for direction and provision. For more information about Groves, see *A. N. Groves* by F.A. Tatford, a booklet available from Echoes of Service, 124 Wells Road, Bath, Avon, BA2 3AH, England or the most recent study by Robert T. Dann, *Father of faith missions: the life and times of Anthony Norris Groves*.

[25] To avoid misunderstanding it should be noted that Henry Martyn consulted Abraham Whelock's translation of the gospels into Persian, which was published in London in 1657. These gospels were found to contain too many Arabic expressions to be of much use. Another attempt which deserves mention is that by Father Leopoldo Sabastiani, who spent many years in Persia as a member of the Roman Catholic mission. His translation of the gospels was printed in very small numbers. According to the long-term missionary in Iran, William McElwee (1892-1993), two original copies of the first 1815 Russian printing (unfortunately containing errors and omissions, probably due to the rush of the production) are treasured by the Christian communities in Shiraz and Tabriz (*My Persian Pilgrimage*, p. 252).

[26] Copies of it can be obtained from Elam Ministries, P.O. Box 75, Godalming, GU8 6YP, England.

[27] In 1865, the Arabic Bible was published in Beirut, Lebanon. The translation by Dr. Eli Smith and Dr. C. Van Dyck followed almost thirty years of patient labour with the valuable co-operation of two Lebanese Christians, Nasif al-Yazeji (1800-1871) and Butrus Bustani (1819-1883).

[28] Available from Light of Life, P.O. Box 13, A-9503 Villach, Austria.

[29] See *Christ in the Art of Husayn Behzad of Iran*, Presbyterian Distribution Service, 225 Vatrick Street, New York, 100014, USA.

EPILOGUE
THOUGH DEAD HE SPEAKS...

What can be learned from Henry's example and experiences?

This brief conclusion to this book is meant to help the reader keep the basic practical content of the study in mind. Though it is almost two centuries since this missionary and translator passed away, and things have changed for the better or the worse in the fields where he laboured, several valuable lessons can be drawn from his life and achievements.

It is true that his ministry was characterised by his personality and abilities to a very large extent, but several features merit our prayerful attention and are worthy of emulation. While his example of devotion to the Lord and dedication to His work should inspire and motivate us, we should not regard him as faultless. Fascination with a person often leads to idealisation and can result in our making him or her more glorious than is really the case. We could point to negative traits in this missionary, but the whole purpose of the study is to show how the Lord used him despite these as He can use anyone who is fully committed to Him.

The following is a summary in five points of this short biography, designed to leave thoughts with the reader that he or she can ponder for practical application in personal Christian testimony and service. 'Consider what I say, and may the Lord give you understanding in all things' (2 Tim. 2:7).

1) To be self-supporting as a chaplain was not contrary to the principle of trusting the Lord for every need (Phil. 4:19). Henry was able to go to overseas missionary fields as a tent-maker (see Acts 18:1-3, 20:34; 1 Thess. 2:9; 2 Thess. 3:7-9) and fulfil his family obligations at the same time (see 1 Tim. 5:8). This is probably the only option for Christian witnesses who desire to settle for shorter or longer periods in Muslim countries today. It also has the benefit of relieving their

brethren at home of some of the burden of supporting them financially.

2) Henry did not allow his strong love for Lydia to hinder him from following God's will for his life, though his renunciation of her remained a painful preoccupation. Such a choice is never easy but we have to remember that it is not enough that an eventual marriage is *in* the Lord (see 1 Cor. 7:39). It should also be *of* the Lord. In all areas of life our preferences must never infringe our obedience to the Lord: '… It is no longer I … but Christ who lives in me …' (Gal. 2:20, see also Ps. 37:4).

3) Henry was willing to bear the reproach of Christ Jesus, the Son of God, in the face of Muslim fanaticism, and endured all the various kinds of difficulties and sufferings involved in this without becoming bitter against his opponents (see Heb. 12:14, 15). It is easy to lose one's self-control and temper before an angry crowd or a scornful Muslim, but whatever the adversity we should not grow bitter but rather seek to display the features of Christ.

4) When Henry's capacity to preach failed him because of illness, he decided to turn his whole attention to translating the New Testament. Limitations and restrictions, physical, political or otherwise that affect one important thing should never become reasons for resignation from all the Lord's work, because there are often other opportunities for using our natural talents and spiritual gifts for the furtherance of the gospel.

5) Henry's close walk with the Lord spoke with greater impact to the people than his preaching. Christian love, forbearance, and a holy life have greater effect among Muslims because they are so used to religious debate, clichés and platitudes that they can become almost immune to argument.

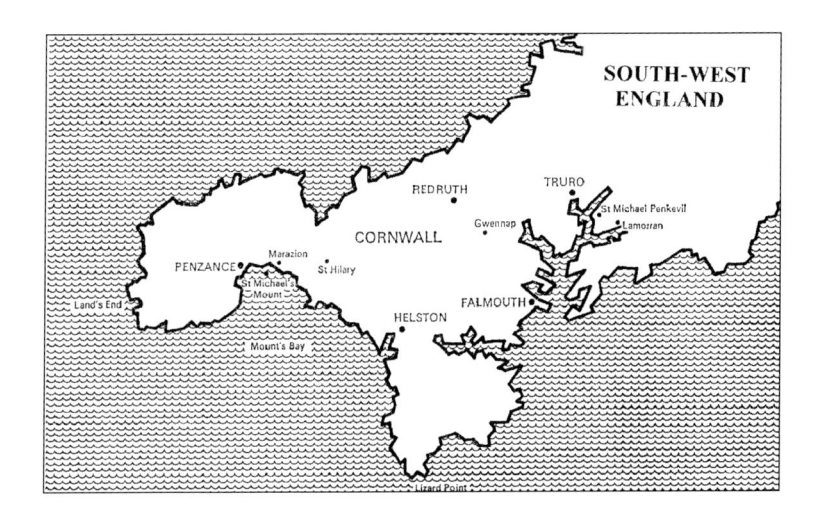

Maps

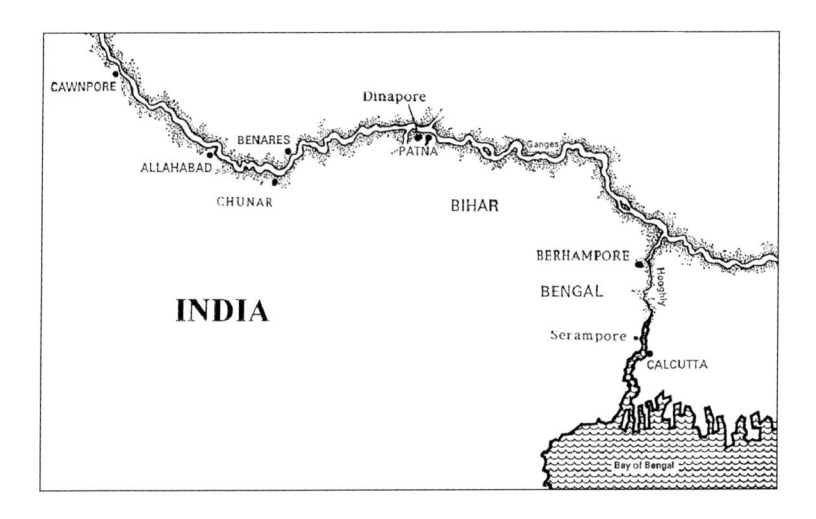

SOUTH-WEST ENGLAND

Land's End, Penzance, St Michael's Mount, Mount's Bay, Marazion, St Hilary, Helston, Lizard Point, Gwennap, Redruth, Truro, St Michael Penkevil, Lamorran, Falmouth, CORNWALL

INDIA

Cawnpore, Allahabad, Chunar, Benares, Patna, Dinapore, Ganges, Bihar, Berhampore, Bengal, Serampore, Hooghly, Calcutta, Bay of Bengal

BLACK SEA
CASPIAN SEA
TOKAT
TURKEY
ERZERUM
EDITERRANEAN SEA
TABRIZ
TURKMENISTAN
IRAQ
TEHRAN
ISFAHAN
AFGHANISTAN
SHIRAZ
BUSHIRE
PERSIAN GULF
PAKISTAN
ARABIA
INDIA
MUSCAT
RED SEA
INDIAN OCEAN
BOMBAY

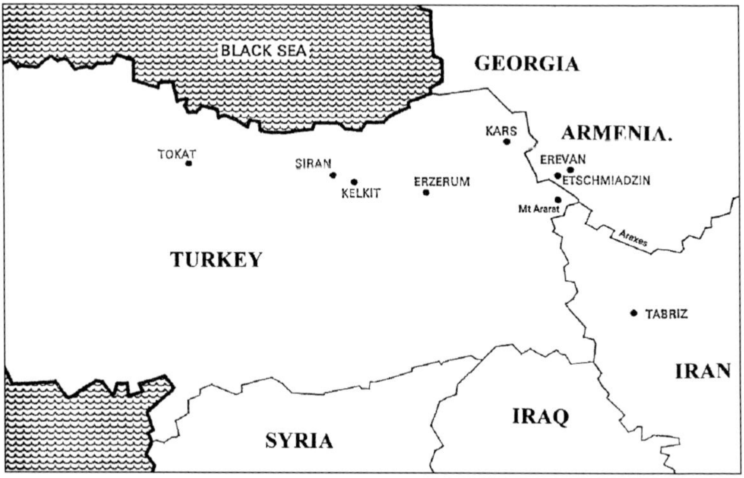
BLACK SEA
GEORGIA
KARS
ARMENIA.
TOKAT
SIRAN
KELKIT
ERZERUM
EREVAN
ETSCHMIADZIN
Mt Ararat
Araxes
TURKEY
TABRIZ
IRAN
IRAQ
SYRIA

BIBLIOGRAPHY

Algar, Hamid — *Religion and state in Iran 1785-1906: the role of the Ulama in the Qajar period.* (Berkeley, CA: University of California Press, 1969)

Bentley-Taylor, D. — *My love must wait: the story of Henry Martyn* (London: Inter-Varsity Fellowship,1975)

Bell, C. — *Henry Martyn* (London: Hodder & Stoughton, 1886)

Butler, E.T. — *The life and work of Henry Martyn, missionary and translator* (Calcutta: Christian Literature Crusade for India, 1922)

Campbell, W. — *The Qur'an and the Bible in the light of history and science* (London: Middle East Resources, 1989)

Cormack, P. — *Wilberforce: the nation's conscience* (Basingstoke: Pickering, 1983)

Corrie, G. E. & H. — *Memoirs of the Right Rev. Daniel Corrie* (London: Burnside & Seeley, 1847)

Cragg, K. — *Troubled by truth: life-studies in inter-faith concern* (Edinburgh: Pentland Press, 1992)

Cromarty, J. — *For the love of India – The story of Henry Martyn* (Darlington: Evangelical Press, 2005)

Dann, R.B. — *Father of faith missions: the life and times of Anthony Norris Groves* (Milton Keynes: Authentic Paternoster, 2004)

Davies, G.C.B.	*The early Cornish evangelicals 1735-60* (London: SPCK, 1951)
Donaldson, D.	*The Shi'ite religion: a history of Islam in Persia and Iraq* (London: SPCK, 1942)
Darton, F.J.H.	*The life and times of Mrs. Sherwood (1775-1851), from the diaries of Captain and Mrs. Sherwood* (London: Wells Gardner, Darton & Co., 1910)
Eaton, B.	*Letters to Lydia – 'Beloved Persis'* (Penzance: Hypatia Publications, 2005)
Edwards, J.	*The life of the Rev. David Brainerd* (Grand Rapids, MI: Baker Book House, 1978)
Eardley, V.	*Henry Martyn* (edited and translated into Persian by Sohail Azeri) (Tehran: Light of the World, 1962)
France, R.T.	*Henry Martyn* in *Five Pioneer Missionaries* (London: Banner of Truth, 1965)
Finnie, K.M.	*Beyond the minarets; a biography of Henry Martyn* (Bromley, Kent: STL Books, 1988)
Frame, H.	*Temperature 129°F: a narrative of Henry Martyn* (London: Edinburgh House Press, 1937)
Gairdner, T.	*The Reproach of Islam* (Westminster: Society for the Gospel in Foreign Parts, 1910)
Goddard, H.	*A history of Christian-Muslim relations* (Edinburgh: Edinburgh University Press, 2000)

Henry, B.V.	*Elsk disse araberne: Gud's lofer blir virkeliggjort* (Ottestad: Prokla-Media, 1997)
Henry, B.V.	*Fra Islam til Golgata* (Oslo: Luther Forlag, 1982)
Henry, B.V.	*Muslims near and far away – challenges and opportunities* (Pikeville, TN: Lighthouse Publishing, 2005)
Hopkins, H.E.	*Charles Simeon of Cambridge* (London: Hodder & Stoughton, 1977)
Howard, David	*Student power in world missions* 2nd ed. (Downers Grove, IL: Inter-Varsity Press, 1979)
Hultvall, J.	*Mission och revolution i Centralasien* (Stockholm: Gummessons,1981)
Jones, L.B.	*People of the mosque* (Calcutta: Baptist Mission Press, 1965, originally published, London: SCM Press, 1932)
Kaye, J.W.	*The life and correspondence of Major-General Sir John Malcolm* 2 vols. (London: Smith, Elder, 1856)
Kaye, J.W.	*Lives of Indian officers* 2 vols. (London: Strahan, 1856)
Kelly, S., ed.	*The Life and Times of Mrs Sherwood … with Extracts from Mr Sherwood's Journal during his Imprisonment in France and Residence in India* (London: Dalton, 1854)

Laird, M.A. ed. Bishop Heber in northern India (London: Cambridge University Press, 1971)

Lang, G.H. Anthony Norris Groves, saint and pioneer: a combined study of a man of God and of the original principles of the Brethren 2nd ed. (London: Paternoster, 1949)

Latourette, K.S. A history of the expansion of Christianity New ed. 7 vols. (Exeter: Paternoster Press, 1971)

Loane, M. Henry Martyn: a star in the Orient in They were pilgrims (Sydney: Angus & Robertson, 1970)

Lopez, A. Henry Martyn: muhammedanernas apostel (Stockholm: Filadelfia Förlaget, 1937)

MacDonald, W. Grasping the shadows (London: Pickering & Inglis, 1978)

Macnaghten, A. Daniel Corrie, his family and friends. (London: Johnson, 1969)

Martyn, H., et al. Controversial tracts on Christianity and Mohammedanism; translated and explained by Samuel Lee. (Cambridge: J. Smith, 1824)

Martyn, H. Sermons (Calcutta: Church Mission Press, 1822)

Martyn, J.R.C. Henry Martyn (1781-1812), Scholar and Missionary to India and Persia: a Biography (Lampeter: Edwin Mellen Press, 1999)

Bibliography

McLean, A.	*Epoch makers of modern missions* (New York: Fleming H. Revell, 1912)
Miller, W.M.	*My Persian pilgrimage* (Pasadena, CA: 1892-1983. William Carey Library, 1989)
Moon, P.	*The British conquest and dominion of India* (London: Duckworth, 1989)
Moule, H.C.G.	*Charles Simeon* (London; Inter-Varsity Fellowship, 1952, originally published 1892)
Neill, S.	*A history of Christian missions* (Harmondsworth: Penguin, 1964)
Padwick, C.	*Henry Martyn: Confessor of the Faith* (London: Inter-Varsity Fellowship, 1963, originally published 1922)
Padwick, C.	*Temple Gairdner of Cairo* (London: Society for Promoting Christian Knowledge, 1929)
Page, J.	*Henry Martyn: pioneer missionary to India and Islam* (Belfast: Ambassador Publications, 2003, reprint of *Henry Martyn of India and Persia* London: Pickering & Inglis, 1930)
Philips, C.H.	*The East India Company, 1784-1834* 2nd ed. (Manchester: Manchester University Press, 1968)
Pollock, J.	*John Wesley* (London: Hodder & Stoughton, 1989)

Potts, E.D.	*British Baptist missionaries in India, 1793-1837* (London: Cambridge University Press, 1967)
Pouncy, A.G.	*Henry Martyn, 1781-1812: the first modern apostle to the Mohammedan* (London: Church Book Room Press, 1947)
Powell, A. A.	*Muslims and missionaries in pre-Mutiny India* (London: Curzon Press, 1993)
Sargent, J.	*A Memoir of the Rev Henry Martyn*, 11th ed. (London: Seeley & Burnside, 183; republished: The Banner of Truth Trust, 1985)
Sargent, J.	*The life of the Rev T T Thomason* (London: Seeley & Burnside, 1833)
Simeon, C.	*The life of the Rev David Brown* (London: Religious Tract Society, 1832)
Smith, G.	*Henry Martyn: Saint and Scholar* (London: Religious Tract Society, 1892)
Stacey, V.	*Life of Henry Martyn* (Hyderabad: Henry Martyn Institute of Islamic Studies, 1980)
Stanley, B.	*The Bible and the flag: Protestant missions and British imperialism in the nineteenth and twentieth centuries* (Leicester: Apollos, 1990)
Stock, E.	*History of the Church Missionary Society*, 4 vols. (London: CMS 1899-1916)

Bibliography

Tatford, F. A.	*The challenge of India* in *That the world may know*, vol. 3 (Bath: Echoes of Service, 1983)
Thornbury, J.	*David Brainerd: pioneer missionary to the American Indians* (Durham: Evangelical Press, 1996)
Titus, M.T.	*Islam in India and Pakistan* (Madras: Christian Literature Society, 1959)
Walker, F.D.	*William Carey, missionary pioneer and statesman* (Chicago: Moody Press, 1951)
Vander Werff, L.	*Christian mission to Muslims: the record* (Pasadena CA: William Carey Library, 1977)
Waterfield, R.E.	*Christians in Persia* (London: Allen & Unwin, 1973)
Wilberforce, S., ed.	*Journals and letters of the Rev Henry Martyn* 2 vols. (London: Seeley & Burnside, 1837)
Wright, Sir D.	*The English amongst the Persians during the Qajar period, 1787-1921* (London: Heinemann, 1977)
Zwemer, S.M.	*Arabia: the Cradle of Islam* (Edinburgh: Oliphant, Anderson & Ferrier, 1900)

Other sources

The original diary of Lydia Grenfell, covering the years 1801-1826, which is held by the Royal Institution of Cornwall, Truro.

INDEX

Abbas Mirza, Prince 111, 114, 115
Abdul Masih (see also Sheikh Saleh) 83, 84, 85, 136
Aldeen 59, 62, 64, 96
Arabia 9, 13, 94, 95, 97, 99, 100, 101, 102, 105, 121, 126, 144
Arabic 71, 74, 89, 90, 91, 93, 94, 95, 100, 101, 104, 108, 118, 121, 137, 139, 140, 141, 142, 148, 152
Bankipore 68
Brainerd, David 11, 23, 24, 25, 26, 33, 56, 99, 126, 132, 139
Brainerd, Thomas 127
Brown, David 59, 62, 63, 64, 68, 73, 74, 82, 83, 84, 86, 88, 96, 97, 98, 104, 126, 168
Bruce, Robert 138, 140
Buchanan, Claudius 59, 60, 66, 74, 98
Bushire 102
Calcutta 12, 23, 38, 39, 43, 49, 54, 58, 59, 61, 62, 63, 64, 66, 68, 69, 74, 80, 83, 90, 91, 94, 95, 96, 97, 98, 99, 104, 136, 140
Cambridge 9, 13, 16, 17, 22, 25, 26, 27, 30, 31, 34, 36, 38, 39, 44, 45, 47, 48, 51, 54, 59, 66, 68, 74, 83, 85, 92, 96, 104, 115, 119, 131, 136, 139, 142, 143, 151
Cardew, Dr Cornelius 16
Carey, William 28, 35, 59, 65, 67, 77, 80
Cawnpore 73, 81, 82, 84, 86, 87, 89, 92, 93, 95, 100, 102, 104, 106, 126, 131
Corrie, Daniel 32, 68, 69, 73, 82, 83, 84, 86, 92, 93, 96, 98, 104, 112, 124, 126, 131, 136, 151
Corrie, Mary 53, 84, 85
Dinapore 64, 68, 69, 71, 72, 73, 74, 77, 79, 81, 86, 87, 91, 92
Dustarjan 103
East India Company 31, 34, 38, 39, 45, 60, 62, 66, 70, 80, 82, 99, 128, 129, 130
Ely Cathedral 36
Emma (cousin) 49
Emma (Lydia's sister) 40
France, Richard T 24, 139
French, Valpy 138
Gairdner, Temple 44
Gilchrist, John B 70, 80
Glen, Dr William 118, 140, 141
Golitsyn, Prince Alexander N 118
Gordon, Peter 147
Grant, Charles 31, 39
Grenfell, Lydia 40, 41, 42, 43, 44, 45, 46, 47, 48, 49, 50, 52, 53, 63, 64, 65, 73, 86, 97, 100, 109, 110, 118, 125, 126, 127, 132, 152, 154, 158, 163, 168
Grenfell, Mary (also 'her mother') 42, 52, 53, 63, 64
Groves, Anthony N 10, 137, 138, 152
Hassan Aga 122, 123
Heber, Reginald 135, 136, 138

Index

Hindi 72
Hindustani 39, 80, 129
Husain Ali Mirza, Prince, 104
India 9, 13, 22, 27, 31, 32, 38, 39, 40, 43, 44, 45, 46, 48, 50, 53, 55, 56, 57, 59, 60, 61, 62, 63, 65, 67, 68, 69, 70, 71, 73, 74, 75, 76, 77, 78, 79, 80, 82, 83, 84, 86, 87, 88, 92, 93, 95, 97, 98, 99, 100, 104, 106, 109, 110, 112, 115, 123, 124, 126, 129, 131, 132, 134, 136, 138, 141, 144, 148, 149, 151
Indian(s) 31, 35, 54, 66, 68, 81, 82, 92, 97, 98, 99, 111
Jaffir Ali Khan 104, 105, 107
Jowett, William J 136, 138
Kay, Sir William 88
Kazen-Beg, Alexander (see also Mirza Muhammad Ali) 118
Keith, Ian 138
Kemp, Dr Johan T van der 56, 57
Kempthorne, John 16, 19, 22
Lee, Samuel 142
MacDonald, William 9
Malcolm, Major-General Sir John 104, 107, 141, 147
Marazion 40, 41, 46, 47, 86
Martyn, John (father) 15, 16, 18, 19, 22, 25, 30
Martyn, John (brother) 16, 35, 84
Martyn, Laura 15, 74, 81
Martyn, Sally 15, 16, 18, 19, 20, 22, 25, 28, 30, 49, 51, 74, 84, 109
McNeill, John 146
Mirza Muhammad Ali (see also Kazen-Beg, Alexander) 118

Mirza Mohammed Fitrus 74, 75, 89, 91
Mirza Said Ali 104, 105, 140
Mohammed Rahim 145, 146
Morier, Isaac 132, 151
Muscat 100, 101, 102
Nehru 38
Newton, Sir Isaac 18, 38
Newton, John 35
Ouseley, Sir Gore 104, 107, 114, 115, 116, 118, 120, 121
Padwick, Constance 149
Patna 68, 72, 75, 106
Persia 9, 13, 62, 70, 75, 77, 78, 79, 80, 84, 94, 95, 97, 99, 100, 101, 102, 103, 104, 107, 108, 111, 112, 115, 119, 121, 123, 127, 138, 144, 146, 147, 149, 152, 168
Persian(s) 62, 70, 71, 74, 78, 83, 84, 89, 90, 93, 94, 100, 102, 103, 104, 110, 111, 113, 114, 118, 119, 121, 122, 128, 129, 140, 142, 143, 144, 147, 148, 151, 152
Persian New Testament 91, 104, 107, 109, 111, 118, 140, 143, 146, 149
Pfander, Karl Gottlieb 144, 145
Rich, Claudius James 128
Sabastiani, Father Leopoldo 152
Sabat, Nathaniel 74, 75, 80, 89, 91, 92, 93, 94, 95, 104, 123, 135, 140
Saleh, Sheikh (see also Abdul Masih) 83
Sargent, John 22, 34, 43, 44, 46, 49, 53, 68, 132, 139, 151, 152,

168
Serampore 59, 65, 68, 80, 111, 140, 141
Sergius 132
Shah Fath Ali Qajar 111, 112
Sherwood, Captain Henry and Mrs Mary 87, 88, 89, 92, 97
Shiraz 102, 103, 104, 105, 106, 107, 108, 110, 111, 113, 114, 116, 119, 124, 140, 146, 152
Simeon, Charles 11, 20, 21, 22, 23, 25, 27, 30, 31, 32, 33, 35, 36, 38, 43, 45, 48, 49, 62, 63, 65, 68, 83, 97, 104, 115, 119, 125, 132, 143, 147, 151
Smith, George 34, 47, 90, 129, 149, 152
Spurgeon, Charles 38
St. John's College, Cambridge 16, 17, 18, 22, 115, 140
St Michael's Mount 47
Tabriz 114, 115, 116, 117, 121, 123, 126, 143, 147, 152
Tehran 104, 113, 114, 118, 140, 141, 146, 147, 151
Thomason, Thomas T 32, 43, 96, 97, 98, 126, 142
Truro 15, 16, 19, 129, 131, 163
Truro Grammar School 16
Turkey 9, 13, 115, 119, 121, 123, 131, 167
Urdu 70, 71, 72, 74, 75, 83, 89, 90, 91, 95, 96, 141, 142, 148
van Lennep, Dr. Henry 128
Verwer, George 9, 11
Wesley, John 16, 20, 22, 26, 29, 31, 131
Whelock, Abraham 152
White, Henry Kirke 22, 23
Wilberforce, William 31, 39
Wilberforce, Samuel 132, 151, 152
Wolff, Joseph 147
Xavier, Francis 62, 80
Young, Major 72
Zagros mountains 103

The author in Istanbul

ABOUT THE AUTHOR

Born into a conservative Roman Catholic family of nine children in Belgium, B V Henry came to a personal faith in Christ at the age of 17 through reading a New Testament given to him by an elderly lady.

During and after his secular education in the 1970's, he developed a strong interest in the spiritual needs of the Muslim world, beginning with Turkey. From that time on, he and his wife have been involved with various evangelistic organisations in several Islamic regions: the Middle East, Central Asia, West Africa, and the Balkans.

Based on his studies and his experiences and tribulations on the field, B V Henry has authored several books in different languages, and regularly writes articles for Christian and secular papers and magazines. His first book printed in

English, *Muslims Near and Far Away*, is now followed by this biography of Henry Martyn, the pioneer-missionary to the Muslims of India and Persia. He has also been intermittently researching and working on his magnum opus, Islam and the West – Reminiscences and Reassessment, which discusses the medieval crusades and their continuing impact on Muslim-Christian relationships.

From the very beginning of his missionary vocation, B V Henry has been eager to share his vision and burden for Muslims. He continues to do so today, as a frequent guest speaker at missionary gatherings and Christian conferences. He also lectures on Islamic topics to evangelical audiences in the United States and elsewhere from his home base in Sweden.

The author would be most grateful to know of any errors in this book which need to be corrected or of any clarifications required for future editions. He would also like to hear from anyone who has found pictures of David Brown, John Sargent and Lydia Grenfell:

B V Henry
PL1232
S-51796 Hultafors
Sweden